www.edudps.com

Jill J. Dixon holds a B.S. in English Education (n Master's Degree in Special Education (summa cum laude). Her teaching experience spans twenty years of working with students in grades K-12, including physically handicapped, emotionally disturbed and learning disabled children. For four years she directed a program which she founded for learning disabled and ADHD children and adolescents. Jill presently operates an Educational Consulting and Testing business and serves as a National Consultant for Home School Legal Defense Association, while home schooling three of her four children. She is the published author of several tests and educational materials.

Mrs. Dixon is available as a conference and workshop speaker on topics such as "ADHD: Fact or Fiction?", "The 5 R's of Homeschooling–What's Really Important?", "The Joy of Learning–Understanding Unique Learning Styles", "Creating Wonderful Writers", and "Assessing Our Children Effectively". Contact her at the address listed below.

DIAGNOSTIC PRESCRIPTIVE SERVICES

www.edudps.com

WRITE WITH THE BEST – Vol. 1

Copyright © 2001 by Jill J. Dixon and T. L. Dixon

ALL RIGHTS RESERVED. No part of this publication may be reproduced or transmitted in any form or by any means, electronic or mechanical, including photocopy, recording, or by any information storage and retrieval system, without prior permission in writing from the publisher and the author.

Printed in U.S.A.

I dedicate this curriculum to my four children, who, by their presence, have always challenged me to do my best!

Special thanks to my oldest son, Evan, for his enthusiastic assistance with the literary passages.

www.edudps.com

TABLE OF CONTENTS

	PAGE
INTRODUCTION	6
HOW TO USE THIS PROGRAM	9
SPECIAL NOTE #1 AND #2	13

UNIT 1: WRITING A DESCRIPTIVE PARAGRAPH – DESCRIBING AN OBJECT — 14
20,000 Leagues Under the Sea
by Jules Verne

UNIT 2: WRITING A DESCRIPTIVE PARAGRAPH – DESCRIBING A PLACE — 20
A Christmas Carol
by Charles Dickens

UNIT 3: WRITING A DESCRIPTIVE PARAGRAPH – DESCRIBING A CHARACTER — 25
Robinson Crusoe
by Daniel Defoe

UNIT 4: WRITING A DIALOGUE — 31
The Wind in the Willows
by Kenneth Grahame

UNIT 5: WRITING A SHORT STORY — 37
"The Gift of the Magi"
by O. Henry

www.edudps.com

		PAGE
UNIT 6:	WRITING A FABLE	50

"The Ants and the Grasshopper"

and

"The Shepherd's Boy and the Wolf"

by Aesop

UNIT 7:	WRITING A FRIENDLY LETTER	55

Treasure Island

by Robert Louis Stevenson

UNIT 8:	WRITING POETRY – RHYMING VERSE	61

"The Daffodils"

by William Wordsworth

UNIT 9:	WRITING POETRY – A BALLAD OR NARRATIVE POEM	66

"Paul Revere's Ride"

by Henry Wadsworth Longfellow

THREE CHARACTERISTICS THAT MAKE THE BEST WRITING *THE BEST* — 75

PROOFREADING CHECKLIST — 76

GRADING CRITERIA — 77

LEARNING STYLES SUGGESTIONS AND OTHER WAYS TO AUGMENT THIS CURRICULUM — 78

	PAGE
ADDITIONAL LITERARY PASSAGES	**80**
FOR MODELING WRITING	

HOW TO WRITE GUIDE — 84
- **HOW TO WRITE A DESCRIPTIVE PARAGRAPH** — 84
- **HOW TO WRITE A DIALOGUE** — 86
- **HOW TO WRITE A SHORT STORY** — 87
- **HOW TO WRITE A FABLE** — 89
- **HOW TO WRITE A FRIENDLY LETTER** — 90
- **HOW TO WRITE RHYMING VERSE** — 92
- **HOW TO WRITE A BALLAD OR NARRATIVE POEM** — 93

ANSWER KEY TO CITED LITERARY PASSAGES — 94

INTRODUCTION

It doesn't take long, when looking in educational arenas – homeschool, public, and private – to discover that writing has been one of the most neglected subjects of our modern educational era. In the state in which I live, mandatory educational reforms have been made to improve the writing skills of students in elementary, middle, and high-school grades. This was finally accomplished because state colleges complained about incoming freshman who were unable to write even a paragraph adequately. The large majority of these students were required to take remedial composition classes before they could enter regular freshman English classes. In twelve to thirteen years of public or private education, they were never taught to write. Unfortunately, I have also seen this trend among homeschooled children. In the writing classes that I teach, I have found that many students have been taught to write sentences and brief paragraphs, but have never moved beyond that point into proficiency in various writing genres. For example, they have no idea how to correctly write a letter, compose poetry or write an essay and have no idea what it means to write *descriptively*. We all know that competent writing is essential in our age of communication and is a huge component of an excellent and complete education.

This curriculum was devised as a result of eighteen years of teaching writing to students in grades K-5 through 12, including public, private, and homeschooled children. Many of the ideas presented in this book were used in a homeschool writing class that I have taught for the last four years. I used classical literature and other great works as models of excellent writing, while teaching students literary appreciation and analysis at the same time. Students were required to bring in weekly samples of "excellent" writing and to be able to explain what made the writing "excellent". They took weekly dictation from the passages and modeled their assignments after these writings. Amazing improvements were made, and many of my students who had been diagnosed as having learning disabilities in written expression began to enjoy writing for the first time in their lives. I also interviewed homeschooling parents who were dissatisfied with the writing curriculums they had used thus far, and I found that they desired a curriculum that taught writing systematically, yet in a simple and clear way. They requested that a guide be included in the curriculum that would provide instructions on exactly how to write specific genres. Many parents also indicated that their students became bored with various curriculums because they did not offer interesting activities, etc. All of these issues have been addressed in this program. In addition to the instructions contained within the curriculum, a helpful "How To Write Guide" is included to assist parents in the teaching of each genre. A chapter entitled "Additional Literary Passages For Modeling Writing" is also included. Both of these make it possible for parents to continue teaching writing by using my approach, even after the initial literary passages are used. The greatest way for students to learn to write is through continued practice, so I have included resources to insure the continuation of writing skills. <u>Proofreading</u> and <u>listening comprehension</u> skills, which are essential to successful writing, <u>are also taught</u>, and all learning styles are accommodated.

The curriculum contains excerpts from great works of world literature regarding the various genres covered. Although all genres for excellent writing are listed in the complete set, each volume stands alone as complete regarding the genres that it contains. Volume 1 naturally begins with the prerequisites of successful writing and progresses until the end of volume 2. Volumes 1 and 2 together cover grades 3 through 12. You are not required to purchase separate books for each grade level. Devised in this way, the curriculum is very cost effective.

§
Focus and Goal

The focus and goal of this writing program are effective and simple. Its purpose is to zero in on the skills that produce excellent writing and to teach students to use these same skills. To accomplish this, the program doesn't abstractly emphasize various grammatical rules for composition, but rather focuses on the *actual skills* of successful, excellent writers and teaches the observation and emulation of these same skills. Grammar is taught in the context of writing, not as a separate subject. The effective method of this curriculum follows in the *literary* steps of writers of great works of world literature, modeling writing after their methods and techniques for successful composition. *In summary, the focus of this program is to teach students to write* **descriptively** *through emulating the actual skills of masters of great writing. The goal of the program is to produce successful writers who know how to write effectively, who know how to proofread their work efficiently, and who know how to properly analyze great literature.*

HOW TO USE THIS PROGRAM

1. This two-volume writing program was designed so that parents could use each volume for a total of 18 weeks (one half of a school year), with each unit taking 2 weeks to complete. However, many parents will want to use this volume for a full year. Students who have never written a short story or dialogue before may need 3-4 weeks to work on perfecting each of these skills. This may also be the case for other genres. The objective is mastery of writing skills – not to rush through each genre in order to move on to the next one. It is *very important* that students master each prerequisite skill before moving on, even if this takes a month or two months. Students can practice and accomplish each skill by writing a few or several examples of the same genre.

2. I highly encourage teachers to have their students write about topics that they are studying in other areas, such as history or science. It is a proven fact that children retain information much better if it is incorporated into as many subjects as possible. An example of this would be to write a friendly letter to Thomas Jefferson, while you are studying The Declaration of Independence or to write a short story about the pyramids in Egypt while you are studying ancient history.

3. Evaluate the writing of your students according to their ages and ability levels. For example, if you have two students (one in 3rd grade and one in 9th), you certainly cannot expect the same quality of writing from both students. A simple descriptive paragraph with 5-6 sentences will suffice for a third grader, but an older student would be expected to write a longer and more detailed paragraph. However, keep in mind that this does not include students with learning difficulties. Regardless of age or grade level, if a student has not learned the elementary skills of writing, evaluate him as a beginner.

4. Each family must have a dictionary and a thesaurus. An English handbook may also be beneficial for parents. Many parents will want to provide additional practice in capitalization, punctuation, English usage and using specific parts of speech. Many excellent English workbooks cover these skills. For students in grades 3-8, I recommend *Daily Grams* and *Easy Grammar.*

5. To thoroughly utilize the "Proofreading Checklist", some students will need instruction in some of the skills addressed in the checklist such as run-on sentences and subject-verb agreement. Any English handbook will cover these, as will most English workbooks. For additional practice with proofreading skills, I recommend *Editor-In-Chief* or *Great Editing Adventures.* However, the best practice for proofreading skills is for students to constantly proofread their own papers, which is an effective feature of WRITE WITH THE BEST.

6. Some students may have difficulty reading the literary passages by themselves. If such is the case, parents should read these to the students while the students follow along. For students who have motor difficulties or problems writing down their thoughts on paper, it is totally acceptable for teachers to write what their students dictate to them. This can be done with each objective that requires writing on the part of the student.

7. One dictation exercise is included in each unit to reinforce the modeling of good writing. Dictation is proven to encourage good listening skills and writing habits, as well as to improve spelling, editing, and usage skills. After taking dictation during each unit, students should then correct their writing *by comparing it* to the literary passage. Students who are not skilled in dictation should begin by taking one sentence of dictation. All other students need not take more than three or four sentences of dictation. However, additional dictation from the literary passages can be given if parents so desire. (Students with motor

difficulties should not be expected to take dictation.)

8. In each unit, students are directed to find another example of the genre they are writing. Many families will have books at home with these examples, but please use your local libraries and librarians to help you if you do not have them available in your home. Plan ahead by looking in the "Table of Contents" at the next genre you will be working on.

9. The teacher should read the objectives of all 10 days of each unit before the student begins so that the progression of the curriculum can be realized. There is a calculated progression in the program. Also, some days are extended into the following days.

10. Teachers must make sure that <u>all</u> of the objectives of each day are achieved so that the goal of this curriculum, mastery of good writing skills, can be realized.

11. Emphasis in the form of **bold** text, *italicized* text, and <u>underscored</u> text is used throughout the book. Each different kind of emphasis is utilized for clarification of each objective so that the student will not miss each important element within each objective. Sometimes emphasis is not repeated when the objectives restate issues.

12. Students should look up the definitions of all unfamiliar words in the literary passages while reading or listening to the passages. This will help improve their vocabulary and comprehension skills. Great works of world literature are excellent for teaching vocabulary. If your student finds any of the passages difficult to understand, realize these passages were chosen to teach vocabulary <u>together with</u> writing skills.

13. Parents are permitted to copy only the pages containing the cited literary passages (also referred to in this curriculum as reading passages) and the "Proofreading Checklist" for their students' use. You will need to make copies of the pages containing the cited literary passages and the "Proofreading Checklist" if you are using the book for more than one student or if you desire to maintain the book un-

marked. Therefore, under such circumstances, making copies of these passages and the "Proofreading Checklist" is not just permitted, but also recommended.

14. An answer key has been provided in the back of this book to verify the student's work concerning the parts of speech and literary elements found in the cited literary passages. <u>Only</u> <u>descriptive</u> adjectives, verbs, adverbs, and <u>specific</u> nouns are listed. <u>Not</u> <u>all</u> nouns, verbs, adjectives, and adverbs are included. Each verb, adjective, and adverb listed is color specified in order to facilitate use of the answer key.

Special Note #1

We have chosen the great works of world literature found in this program because of their incomparable descriptions, themes, characters, and their styles of writing. Even though their authors were excellent writers, some of them at times did <u>not</u> follow a number of our modern rules for punctuation and sentence structure or utilize our modern models for writing paragraphs and friendly letters. Therefore, we have corrected some of the punctuation and sentence structure in the literary passages, but have not changed any of the paragraph structure or the friendly letter. When teaching your students, please point out to them that we are modeling these writers because of their content, style and *primarily* their superb descriptive skills. When they depart from our modern rules of punctuation and structure, we will follow the proper requirements as stated in the "How To Write Guide" and your English handbook or workbook. In summary, our aim is to combine the best of both worlds – superlative writing style and correct writing form.

Special Note #2

We have not changed the spelling in the various literary passages cited. We have reproduced the spelling as rendered by each author.

www.edudps.com

UNIT 1
WRITING A DESCRIPTIVE PARAGRAPH - DESCRIBING AN OBJECT

Please Note: For students who have never been taught how to write descriptively using adjectives, verbs, and adverbs, you may want to take longer than two weeks per unit to fully teach and emphasize this very important skill.

I highly recommend *Easy Grammar* by Wanda Phillips for students who need extra practice understanding nouns, verbs, adjectives, and adverbs. These parts of speech must be mastered in order to learn how to write descriptively.

Day 1 3 Objectives (each objective is indicated by an asterisk)

*Read this passage from 20,000 Leagues Under the Sea by Jules Verne.

I looked in my turn, and could not repress a gesture of disgust. Before my eyes was a horrible monster worthy to figure in the legends of the marvellous. It was an immense cuttlefish, being eight yards long. It swam crossways in the direction of the Nautilus with great speed, watching us with its enormous staring green eyes. Its eight arms, or rather feet, fixed to its head, that have given the name of cephalopod to these animals, were twice as long as its body, and were twisted like the furies' hair. One could see the 250 air holes on the inner side of the tentacles. The monster's mouth, a horned beak like a parrot's, opened and shut vertically. Its tongue, a horned substance, furnished with several rows of pointed teeth, came out quivering from this veritable pair of shears. What a freak of nature, a bird's beak on a mollusc! Its spindle-like body formed a fleshy mass that might weigh 4,000 to 5,000 lbs.; the varying colour changing with great rapidity, according to the irritation of the animal, passed successively from livid grey to reddish brown. What irritated this mollusc? No doubt the presence of the Nautilus, more formidable than itself, and on which its suckers or its jaws had no hold. Yet, what monsters these poulps are! What vitality the Creator has given them! What vigour in their movements! And they possess three hearts! Chance had brought us in presence of this cuttlefish, and I did not wish to lose the opportunity of carefully studying this specimen of cephalopods. I overcame the horror that inspired me, and, taking a pencil, began to draw it.

(*Parents, discuss with your student *why* he/she thinks this passage is an example of "good" writing.)

*Read "Three Characteristics that Make the Best Writing *The Best*" on page 75.

Day 2 4 Objectives

*Learn these *parts of speech* meanings:

    Noun: a person, place, or thing

    Verb: a word that shows an action (It is not necessary to discuss linking verbs at this time.)

Adjective: a word that describes a noun

> An **adjective** answers these questions about a noun: *Which one? What kind? How much? How many?*

Adverb: a word that describes mainly a verb, but also an adjective and other adverbs

> An **adverb** answers these questions about verbs, adjectives, and other adverbs: *When? Where? How? To what extent? (how much or how long?)*

*Review characteristic #2 from "Three Characteristics that Make the Best Writing *The Best*". *Discuss with the student the meanings of **nouns**, **verbs**, **adjectives** and **adverbs** and their importance in descriptive writing.

*Write your own examples of **nouns**, **verbs**, **adjectives**, and **adverbs**. Name at least *five examples* for each one.

Day 3 2 Objectives

*Review the meanings of *parts of speech* from yesterday.

> Note: Descriptive adjectives, verbs, and adverbs create pictures in the reader's mind. Descriptive verbs are action verbs and do not include linking verbs such as *are, is, was, were, be, being,* and *been*.
>
> Specific nouns also paint word pictures by giving particular and concrete details that readers can visualize.

*Underline each *descriptive* **adjective** in red, each *descriptive* **verb** in green, and each *descriptive* **adverb** in blue in the reading passage. Also, circle each *specific* **noun**.

(See the Answer Key to verify the student's work.)

(Parents, younger students [Grades 3-5] and students who do not have experience using descriptive parts of speech should not be expected to find every descriptive adjective, verb, adverb, and specific noun. If they find some, this is sufficient.)

Day 4 3 Objectives

*Complete the following exercise using a *thesaurus*. (Parents, this is a good time to explain the purpose of a thesaurus to the student and to teach him to use it.)
*Replace the following **nouns, verbs, adjectives,** and **adverbs** with more *specific* and *descriptive words*. **Nouns** should be *specific* rather than generic. For example, instead of just saying "car", you could say "Chevy" or "limousine".

Replace each word with at least 3 substitute words. *Write these words down.

1. walk
2. see
3. little
4. slowly
5. hungry
6. house
7. quickly
8. nice
9. give
10. street

Day 5 5 Objectives

Now that you know what specific and descriptive **parts of speech** a *descriptive* paragraph should include, *look in a book by a well-known author that you have in your house and find an example of a descriptive paragraph describing an <u>object</u>. *Write down all of the *descriptive* words that you can find. *Close your eyes* and have your teacher read the passage to you. Can you virtually *see* the object? Can you *feel* it? Can you *hear* it? Can you *taste* it? Can you *smell* it? *Take dictation from your teacher from the book you chose or from the reading passage in this unit. *Correct your dictation by comparing it to the book or passage.

Day 6   1 Objective

(*Parents, discuss with your student the following *requirements* for an adequate paragraph.)
Learn these five requirements:
1. It must contain a *topic sentence* – a sentence that tells what the whole paragraph will be about. This sentence is usually the first sentence in a paragraph.
2. The paragraph should contain at least *5 sentences* and preferably more.
3. The *first line* of each paragraph must be *indented*.
4. The *middle sentences* should number at least *3* and must *prove* or *support* the topic sentence.
5. The *last sentence*, called a *concluding sentence*, should basically *restate* the topic sentence, but in different words.

Day 7   2 Objectives

*Each student must come up with an *object* to describe in a *descriptive paragraph*. Choose an object that you have observed or know something about. Choose an object other than the one from the reading passage in this unit. *After reviewing the style of Jules Verne in his description – the way he described his object – write down as many *descriptive* **adjectives**,

verbs, and **adverbs** as you can think of to describe your object. Write down some *specific* **nouns** also. If your object is like his, try not to use the actual words that he used to describe his object, but come up with your own descriptive words instead. Remember that you are to *paint word pictures* so that someone can close their eyes and virtually see, hear, smell, taste, or feel what you are describing when they hear your paragraph read to them. You will complete your paragraph tomorrow.

Day 8 3 Objectives

*First, write your topic sentence for your paragraph that you prepared for yesterday. Make sure it tells what your whole paragraph will be about. For example: "My pet gerbil is a beautiful, interesting creature." *Next, write your paragraph containing at least 5 sentences, with at least 3 sentences which support your topic sentence. *Last, write your concluding sentence.

Day 9 2 Objectives

*Proofread your paragraph by using the proofreading checklist in the back of this book. *<u>Underline</u> all *descriptive* **verbs** in green, *descriptive* **adjectives** in red, and *descriptive* **adverbs** in blue and circle each *specific* **noun**. Make sure you have at least two verbs, two adjectives, and two adverbs, and that at least some of your nouns are *specific*.

Day 10 2 Objectives

*Rewrite or type your paragraph. Make sure all your corrections are made. *Keep your completed paper in a folder to serve as your writing portfolio.

UNIT 2
WRITING A DESCRIPTIVE PARAGRAPH - DESCRIBING A PLACE

Day 1 2 Objectives (each objective is indicated by an asterisk)

*Read the following passages from A Christmas Carol by Charles Dickens.

Once upon a time - of all the good days in the year, on Christmas Eve - old Scrooge sat busy in his counting-house. It was cold, bleak, biting weather, foggy withal, and he could hear the people in the court outside, go wheezing up and down, beating their hands upon their breasts, and stamping their feet upon the pavement stones to warm them. The city clocks had only just gone three, but it was quite dark already - it had not been light all day - and candles were flaring in the windows of the neighbouring offices, like ruddy smears upon the palpable brown air. The fog came pouring in at every chink and keyhole, and was so dense without, that although the court was of the narrowest, the houses opposite were mere phantoms. To see the dingy cloud come drooping down, obscuring everything, one might have thought that Nature lived hard by, and was brewing on a large scale.

§

Meanwhile, the fog and darkness thickened so, that people ran about with flaring links, proffering their services to go before horses in carriages, and conduct them on their way. The ancient tower of a church, whose gruff old bell was always peeping slily down at Scrooge out of a Gothic window in the wall, became invisible, and struck the hours and quarters in the clouds, with tremulous vibrations afterwards as if its teeth were chattering in its frozen head up there. The cold became intense. In the main street at the corner of the court, some labourers were repairing the gas-pipes, and had lighted a great fire in a brazier, round which a party of ragged men and boys were gathered, warming their hands and winking their eyes before the blaze in rapture. The waterplug being left in solitude, its overflowing sullenly congealed, and turned to misanthropic ice. The brightness of the shops where holly sprigs and berries crackled in the lamp heat of the windows, made pale faces ruddy as they passed.

*From what you've previously learned, talk about all of the characteristics that make these passages examples of "good" writing.

Day 2 4 Objectives

*Review the meanings of **nouns**, **verbs**, **adjectives**, and **adverbs**.
*Underline all *descriptive* **verbs** in green, **adjectives** in red, and **adverbs** in blue in the reading passages. (Parents, give examples for review, if

needed.) *Circle *specific* **nouns**.

(See the Answer Key to verify the student's work.)

*Notice the way Dickens gives personal (human) qualities to "Nature" and "the old bell" in the ancient tower. We will cover this use of figurative language in Unit 8.

Day 3   3 Objectives

**Look carefully* at what the author does to make you feel you are actually in this place. *What *senses* does he appeal to? Does he appeal to *sight*, *smell*, *taste*, *touch*, and *hearing*?

*Make a list of each of these senses found in the reading passages.

For example, under "sight" list all the words that Dickens used that have to do with seeing.

Day 4   3 Objectives

*Think of a place that you would like to describe. Visit this place if you can. *Write down as many descriptive words as you can think of to describe this place to someone *who has never been there before*. *Pretend that someone else you know cannot see – what words would you need to vividly describe this place to him? How would you explain the place to make it come alive for him? Think about someone who cannot hear – how would you vividly describe this place to him in writing? Make a list of these vivid words.

Day 5   5 Objectives

*Look in the books that you have at home to find a description of a place. **Why* or *why not* is this a good example of a description of a place? Give as many reasons as you can why this is so. *Note the descriptive words the author uses or come up with words that he could have used in his description. *Take dictation from the reading passages in this unit. *Correct your dictation by comparing it to the passages.

Day 6 (Note: This will be a 2 day assignment.) 2 Objectives

*Remembering what you learned from Day 2 about Mr. Dickens' use of descriptive words and from Day 3 about his method of describing a place, begin writing your paragraph. When writing your topic sentence for your descriptive paragraph of a place, remember to make sure that it tells what your whole paragraph will be about. (Review the rules for writing a paragraph from Unit 1 if you need to.) Remember that an adequate paragraph should have at least 5 sentences, but it certainly can have more. *Make this a *longer paragraph* so that you can *adequately describe* your place.

Day 7 2 Objectives

*Finish your paragraph and *add your concluding sentence.

Day 8 2 Objectives

*Read through your paragraph and underline all *descriptive* **verbs** in green, **adjectives** in red, **adverbs** in blue, and circle all *specific* **nouns**. You should have at least two of each. *If you do not have enough, use your thesaurus to add more.

Day 9 1 Objective

*Use the Proofreading Checklist at the end of this book to "fine tune" your paragraph and make all needed corrections.

Day 10 3 Objectives

*Write or type your final draft. *Read it to your family. *Place your paper in your writing portfolio.

UNIT 3
WRITING A DESCRIPTIVE PARAGRAPH - DESCRIBING A CHARACTER

Day 1 2 Objectives (each objective is indicated by an asterisk)

*Read this passage from <u>Robinson Crusoe</u> by Daniel Defoe.

He was a comely, handsome fellow, perfectly well made, with straight, strong limbs, not too large, tall and well shaped; and, as I reckon, about twenty-six years of age. He had a very good countenance, not a fierce and surly aspect, but seemed to have something very manly in his face; and yet he had all the sweetness and softness of a European in his countenance too, especially when he smiled. His hair was long and black, not curled like wool; his forehead very high and large; and a great vivacity and sparkling sharpness in his eyes. The color of the skin was not quite black, but very tawny; and yet not an ugly, yellow, nauseous tawny, as the Brazilians and Virginians, and other natives of America are, but of a bright kind of a dun-olive color, that had in it something very agreeable, though not very easy to describe. His face was round and plump, his nose small, a very good mouth, thin lips, and his fine teeth well set, and as white as ivory.

After he had slumbered, rather than slept, about half an hour, he awoke again, and came out of the cave to me; for I had been milking my goats, which I had in the inclosure just by. When he espied me, he came running to me, laying himself down again upon the ground, with all the possible signs of an humble, thankful disposition, making a great many antic gestures to show it. At last he laid his head flat upon the ground, close to my foot, and set my other foot upon his head, as he had done before; and after this, made all the signs to me of subjection, servitude, and submission imaginable, to let me know how he would serve me so long as he lived. I understood him in many things, and let him know I was very well pleased with him.

In a little time I began to speak to him, and teach him to speak to me; and, first, I let him know his name should be FRIDAY, which was the day I saved his life. I called him so for the memory of the time. I likewise taught him to say "Master" and then let him know that was to be my name. I likewise taught him to say, "Yes" and "No" and to know the meaning of them. I gave him some milk in an earthen pot, and let him see me drink it before him, and sop my bread in it; and I gave him a cake of bread to do the like, which he quickly complied with, and made signs that it was very good for him. I kept there with him all night, but as soon as it was day, I beckoned to him to come with me, and let him know I would give him some clothes, at which he seemed very glad, for he was stark naked.

Why do you think this passage is considered part of a great work of literature? Name all of the reasons you can think of.

Day 2 4 Objectives

*Have your teacher read the literary passage to you out loud. *Listen carefully for *specific* **nouns** and *descriptive* **adjectives**, **adverbs**, and **verbs**. *Close your eyes* while you are listening and *see if you can visualize* the character being described. *After you hear the passage read aloud, write down *everything you remember* about Friday, the servant, whom Daniel Defoe describes in this passage from Robinson Crusoe. Don't refer to the passage while completing this objective.
(See the Answer Key to verify the student's work.)

Day 3 5 Objectives

*Looking at your list from yesterday, think about how this author *described* his character.
Refer to the literary passage, if necessary, in order to complete the following objectives:
What physical characteristics does this character have? What does he look like?
*What *actions* of the character are described?
*What do you think this author is *saying* about his character? In other words, what does he want his readers to know and think about his character?
*In your own words, write down 3 to 5 sentences describing Friday's personality. Use your thesaurus to come up with *descriptive* words if you need to.

Day 4 5 Objectives

*Make up a fictional (not real) character that you would like to write about in a short story – a character that would be the *main character* in your story.

*Make a list containing as many **adjectives** as you can think of to *describe* this character. Use adjectives that describe his appearance, his attitude, his family, his hobbies or anything about him.
(Note: Review the meaning of adjectives, if necessary.)

*Use your thesaurus and add one word for every **adjective** that you listed.

*Make a list containing as many **verbs** or **action words** with **adverbs** that you can think of to *describe* this character. For example:
- He *listened intently* or *attentively* (to every word spoken to him.)
- He *sincerely loved* (his family.)

(Note: Review the meanings of verbs and adverbs if necessary.)

*Use your thesaurus and add one word for every **verb** and one word for every **adverb** that you listed.

Day 5 3 Objectives

*Using your words and phrases from yesterday, write down 5 sentences to *describe* your character. *Close your eyes* and have someone read these sentences *out loud*. *Can you *picture* this character being described in a *detailed* way? Is he before your eyes as alive in a *vivid* way? If you answered "no", then rewrite your sentences until you can answer "yes".

Day 6 5 Objectives

*Look in the fictional books and novels by other well-known authors that you have at home. *Find another description of a character. *Make lists of the **adjectives**, **verbs**, and **adverbs** that this author used. If you like some of his words, *consider adding them to your description of your character.*

*Have your teacher give you at least one sentence for dictation from either this book or the reading passage from Robinson Crusoe.

*Correct your dictation by comparing it to the book or passage.

Day 7 4 Objectives

*Write a *topic sentence* for your character description. Remember that this sentence **must introduce** your *entire paragraph*. Your readers **must** be able to tell what your *whole paragraph* will be *about* from this *topic sentence*.

*Next, write your paragraph containing *word pictures* to *describe your character*. Refer to your sentences from Day 5 and any additional descriptive words from Day 6. Remember to include your *support sentences* and *end with your *concluding sentence*.

Day 8 4 Objectives

*Underline all *descriptive* **adjectives** in red, **verbs** in green, and **adverbs** in blue in your paragraph. *Make sure that some of your **nouns** are *specific*.

*Do you feel like you have adequately described your character?

*How does your description compare with Daniel Defoe's description of his character? If you feel like it is inadequate, use Mr. Defoe's writing style and rewrite your paragraph using your own words to describe your character.

Day 9 2 Objectives

*Today use the proofreading checklist to proofread your paper. *Make all necessary corrections.

Day 10 2 Objectives

*Write or type your final draft. *Place this in your portfolio. We will use it in our next unit.

UNIT 4
WRITING A DIALOGUE

Day 1   2 Objectives (each objective is indicated by an asterisk)

*Read this passage and dialogue from <u>The Wind in the Willows</u> by Kenneth Grahame. *Pay <u>close</u> <u>attention</u> to *punctuation marks* such as *commas, quotation marks, periods,* and *question marks*.
Note: In the use of dialogue, a separate paragraph is made each time a person speaks. A topic and concluding sentence are not needed in these dialogue paragraphs.

When supper was really finished at last, and each animal felt that his skin was now as tight as was decently safe, and that by this time he didn't care a hang for anybody or anything, they gathered round the glowing embers of the great wood fire, and thought how jolly it was to be sitting up SO late, and SO independent, and SO full; and after they had chatted for a time about things in general, the Badger said heartily, "Now then! tell us the news from your part of the world. How's old Toad going on?"

"Oh, from bad to worse," said the Rat gravely, while the Mole, cocked up on a settle and basking in the firelight, his heels higher than his head, tried to look properly mournful. "Another smash-up only last week, and a bad one. You see, he will insist on driving himself, and he's hopelessly incapable. If he'd only employ a decent, steady, well-trained animal, pay him good wages, and leave everything to him, he'd get on all right. But no; he's convinced he's a heaven-born driver, and nobody can teach him anything; and all the rest follows."

"How many has he had?" inquired the Badger gloomily.

"Smashes, or machines?" asked the Rat. "Oh, well, after all, it's the same thing--with Toad. This is the seventh. As for the others--you know that coach-house of his? Well, it's piled up--literally piled up to the roof--with fragments of motor-cars, none of them bigger than your hat! That accounts for the other six--so far as they can be accounted for."

"He's been in hospital three times," put in the Mole, "and as for the fines he's had to pay, it's simply awful to think of."

"Yes, and that's part of the trouble," continued the Rat. "Toad's rich, we all know; but he's not a millionaire. And he's a hopelessly bad driver and quite regardless of law and order. Killed or ruined--it's got to be one of the two things, sooner or later. Badger! we're his friends--oughtn't we to do something?"

The Badger went through a bit of hard thinking. "Now look here!" he said at last, rather severely. "Of course you know I can't do anything NOW?"

His two friends assented, quite understanding his point. No animal, according to the rules of animal-etiquette, is ever expected to do anything strenuous, or heroic, or even moderately active during the off-season of winter. All are sleepy—some actually asleep. All are weather-bound, more or less; and all are resting from arduous days and nights, during which every muscle in them has been severely tested, and every energy kept at full stretch.

"Very well then!" continued the Badger. "BUT, when once the year has really turned, and the nights are shorter, and halfway through them one rouses and feels fidgety and wanting to be up and doing by sunrise, if not before--YOU know!----" Both animals nodded gravely. THEY knew!

"Well, THEN," went on the Badger, "we--that is, you and me and our friend the Mole here--we'll take Toad seriously in hand. We'll stand no nonsense whatever. We'll bring him back to reason, by force if need be. We'll MAKE him be a sensible Toad."

Day 2 2 Objectives

*Have your teacher read the literary passage out loud to you. *After hearing the passage read to you (more than once if necessary), complete the following about the dialogue:

  1. <u>How</u> does the author *introduce* his dialogue? What does he say be-

fore his characters talk?

2. <u>What</u> do you find out *about the characters* who are talking?

3. <u>What</u> do you find out *about what is happening* in the story or the *events that are taking place?*

4. <u>What</u> do you discover about the characters from *the way they talk* as revealed in the author's use of *descriptive* **parts of speech** and punctuation?

5. <u>Underline</u> all *descriptive language* in this passage.

6. <u>Circle</u> all *specific nouns* in the passage.

7. Put brackets [ ] around any **adverbs** that Mr. Grahame uses to tell how the characters speak. For example: "Get out!" he said **angrily**.

(See the Answer Key to verify the student's work.)

Day 3 4 Objectives

*Read over the rules for writing a dialogue in the "How To Write Guide" at the end of this book. *Study the examples in the "How To Write Guide" carefully and *look again at the reading passage on Day 1, paying <u>close attention</u> to *commas, quotation marks, periods,* and *question marks.*

<u>Where</u> do the *commas* go?

<u>Where</u> do *periods* and *question marks* go?

Do they go <u>inside</u> or <u>outside</u> of the *quotation marks*?

*<u>What</u> do you do *each time a new person speaks*?

Day 4 3 Objectives

*Reviewing the rules from yesterday, write four (4) sentences:

2 of what you have said to people so far today and

2 sentences of what they said back to you.

Write this as a 4-sentence *dialogue*. *<u>Make</u> <u>sure</u> that you follow the rules

for writing a dialogue.
*Proofread your sentences.

Day 5   3 Objectives

*Get out the descriptive paragraph that you wrote about your character from the last unit (Unit 3) and think about a *dialogue* that this character would be in. *Come up with one character or two characters that he would carry on a conversation with. *Write down what you would like to say about these characters through your dialogue. How do you want them to speak to each other? Are they kind, angry, irritated, or frightened? Will they use *Standard English* or speak in a *certain dialect*? What are their personalities like?

Day 6   5 Objectives

*Look in a novel or fictional book by a well-known author that you have in your house and find a *dialogue* in this book. Note any *descriptive language and *different dialect, writing down some examples of these that you may want to use in your dialogue.
*Have your teacher dictate some sentences to you from this book or from the reading passage from Day 1. *Correct your dictation by comparing it to the book or passage.

Day 7   5 Objectives

*As you consider the ways that Kenneth Grahame wrote about his characters' conversations, use them as clues and write your dialogue between your characters. *Use your thesaurus to find *descriptive* **verbs** to use instead of the word "said". *Use it to find *vivid* **adverbs** to use with your verbs. *Also use appropriate punctuation in your descriptive dialogue.

*Make sure you also use descriptive language in your sentences that come <u>before</u> your dialogue. Remember that *these sentences* are also <u>very important</u>.

Day 8   3 Objectives

*Have someone read your dialogue out loud to you <u>twice</u>. **Listen carefully* for *descriptive language* and *clues* about your characters. *Make all necessary additions and corrections.

Day 9   2 Objectives

*Proofread your dialogue for *punctuation, capitalization,* and *complete sentences.* *<u>Pay close attention</u> to the placement of <u>commas</u>, <u>quotation marks</u>, and <u>ending</u> <u>punctuation</u>. See the "How To Write Guide" for help.

Day 10   2 Objectives

*Write or type your final copy of your dialogue. *Place this in your writing portfolio.

UNIT 5

WRITING A SHORT STORY

Note: This unit will probably take more than 2 weeks for total mastery.

Day 1 2 Objectives (each objective is indicated by an asterisk)

*Read the short story "The Gift of the Magi" by O. Henry and *look for these elements of a short story:

1. *Characters*: Who your story is about – the most important people or objects in the story.
2. *Setting*: When and where the story takes place – the time and place of the story.
3. *Theme*: The message or purpose of the story, such as love, courage, obedience, or making the right choice.
4. *Plot*: How your story happens – the things that happen in a story – the series of events.
   This also includes: (a) the conflict or problem – every story has a problem that arises (b) the climax or turning point – this is the biggest thing that happens or where everything changes (usually for the better) (c) the resolution – how the conflict or problem is solved.
5. *Narrator* or *Point of View*: This can be: 1st Person – "I", 2nd Person – "You" (this is rarely used), 3rd Person – "She", "They", "He", "Them" (3rd Person is what is used most often in short stories. The narrator is telling the story about someone else.)
6. *Dialogue*: Almost all short stories contain conversation (dialogue) between important characters.
7. *Tone*: The author's outlook or attitude toward what he is writing about. Is he serious, angry, respectful, happy, etc.?

THE GIFT OF THE MAGI

One dollar and eighty-seven cents. That was all. And sixty cents of it was in pennies. Pennies saved one and two at a time by bulldozing the grocer and the vegetable man and the butcher until one's cheeks burned with the silent imputation of parsimony that such close dealing implied. Three times Della counted it. One dollar and eighty-seven cents. And the next day would be Christmas.

There was clearly nothing to do but flop down on the shabby little couch and howl. So Della did it. Which instigates the moral reflection that life is made up of sobs, sniffles, and smiles, with sniffles predominating.

While the mistress of the home is gradually subsiding from the first stage to the second, take a look at the home. A furnished flat at $8 per week. It did not exactly beggar description, but it certainly had that word on the lookout for the mendicancy squad.

In the vestibule below was a letter-box into which no letter would go, and an electric button from which no mortal finger could coax a ring. Also appertaining thereunto was a card bearing the name "Mr. James Dillingham Young."

The "Dillingham" had been flung to the breeze during a

former period of prosperity when its possessor was being paid $30 per week. Now, when the income was shrunk to $20, though, they were thinking seriously of contracting to a modest and unassuming D. But whenever Mr. James Dillingham Young came home and reached his flat above he was called "Jim" and greatly hugged by Mrs. James Dillingham Young, already introduced to you as Della. Which is all very good.

Della finished her cry and attended to her cheeks with the powder rag. She stood by the window and looked out dully at a gray cat walking a gray fence in a gray backyard. Tomorrow would be Christmas Day, and she had only $1.87 with which to buy Jim a present. She had been saving every penny she could for months, with this result. Twenty dollars a week doesn't go far. Expenses had been greater than she had calculated. They always are. Only $1.87 to buy a present for Jim. Her Jim. Many a happy hour she had spent planning for something nice for him. Something fine and rare and sterling-- something just a little bit near to being worthy of the honor of being owned by Jim.

There was a pier-glass between the windows of the room. Perhaps you have seen a pierglass in an $8 flat. A very thin and very agile person may, by observing his reflection in a rapid sequence of longitudinal strips, obtain a fairly accurate conception of his looks. Della, being slender, had mastered the art.

Suddenly she whirled from the window and stood before the glass. Her eyes were shining brilliantly, but her face had lost its color within twenty seconds. Rapidly she pulled down her hair and let it fall to its full length.

Now, there were two possessions of the James Dillingham Youngs in which they both took a mighty pride. One was Jim's gold watch that had been his father's and his grandfather's. The other was Della's hair. Had the queen of Sheba lived in the flat across the airshaft, Della would have let her hair hang out the window some day to dry just to depreciate Her Majesty's jewels and gifts. Had King Solomon been the janitor, with all his treasures piled up in the basement, Jim would have pulled out his watch every time he passed, just to see him pluck at his beard from envy.

So now Della's beautiful hair fell about her rippling and shining like a cascade of brown waters. It reached below her knee and made itself almost a garment for her. And then she did it up again nervously and quickly. Once she faltered for a minute and stood still while a tear or two splashed on the worn red carpet.

On went her old brown jacket; on went her old brown hat.

With a whirl of skirts and with the brilliant sparkle still in her eyes, she fluttered out the door and down the stairs to the street.

Where she stopped the sign read: "Mne. Sofronie. Hair Goods of All Kinds." One flight up Della ran, and collected her self, panting. Madame, large, too white, chilly, hardly looked the "Sofronie."

"Will you buy my hair?" asked Della.

"I buy hair," said Madame. "Take yer hat off and let's have a sight at the looks of it."

Down rippled the brown cascade.

"Twenty dollars," said Madame, lifting the mass with a practised hand.

"Give it to me quick," said Della.

Oh, and the next two hours tripped by on rosy wings. Forget the hashed metaphor. She was ransacking the stores for Jim's present.

She found it at last. It surely had been made for Jim and

no one else. There was no other like it in any of the stores, and she had turned all of them inside out. It was a platinum fob chain simple and chaste in design, properly proclaiming its value by substance alone and not by meretricious ornamentation--as all good things should do. It was even worthy of The Watch. As soon as she saw it she knew that it must be Jim's. It was like him. Quietness and value--the description applied to both. Twenty-one dollars they took from her for it, and she hurried home with the 87 cents. With that chain on his watch Jim might be properly anxious about the time in any company. Grand as the watch was, he sometimes looked at it on the sly on account of the old leather strap that he used in place of a chain.

When Della reached home her intoxication gave way a little to prudence and reason. She got out her curling irons and lighted the gas and went to work repairing the ravages made by generosity added to love. Which is always a tremendous task, dear friends--a mammoth task.

Within forty minutes her head was covered with tiny, close-lying curls that made her look wonderfully like a truant schoolboy. She looked at her reflection in the mirror long, carefully, and critically.

"If Jim doesn't kill me," she said to herself, "before he takes a second look at me, he'll say I look like a Coney Island chorus girl. But what could I do--oh! what could I do with a dollar and eighty-seven cents?"

At 7 o'clock the coffee was made and the frying-pan was on the back of the stove hot and ready to cook the chops.

Jim was never late. Della doubled the fob chain in her hand and sat on the corner of the table near the door that he always entered. Then she heard his step on the stair away down on the first flight, and she turned white for just a moment. She had a habit for saying little silent prayer about the simplest everyday things, and now she whispered: "Please God, make him think I am still pretty."

The door opened and Jim stepped in and closed it. He looked thin and very serious. Poor fellow, he was only twenty-two--and to be burdened with a family! He needed a new overcoat and he was without gloves.

Jim stopped inside the door, as immovable as a setter at the scent of quail. His eyes were fixed upon Della, and there was an expression in them that she could not read, and it terrified her. It was not anger, nor surprise, nor disapproval, nor horror, nor any of the sentiments that she had been prepared for. He simply stared at her fixedly with that peculiar expression on his face.

Della wriggled off the table and went for him.

"Jim, darling," she cried, "don't look at me that way. I had my hair cut off and sold because I couldn't have lived through Christmas without giving you a present. It'll grow out again-- you won't mind, will you? I just had to do it. My hair grows awfully fast. Say 'Merry Christmas!' Jim, and let's be happy. You don't know what a nice-- what a beautiful, nice gift I've got for you."

"You've cut off your hair?" asked Jim, laboriously, as if he had not arrived at that patent fact yet, even after the hardest mental labor.

"Cut it off and sold it," said Della. "Don't you like me just as well, anyhow? I'm me without my hair, ain't I?"

Jim looked about the room curiously.

"You say your hair is gone?" he said, with an air almost of idiocy.

"You needn't look for it," said Della. "It's sold, I tell you-- sold and gone, too. It's Christmas Eve, boy. Be good to me, for it went for you. Maybe the hairs of my head were numbered," she went on with sudden serious sweetness, "but nobody could ever count my love for you. Shall I put the chops on, Jim?"

Out of his trance Jim seemed quickly to wake. He enfolded his Della. For ten seconds let us regard with discreet scrutiny some inconsequential object in the other direction. Eight dollars a week or a million a year--what is the difference? A mathematician or a wit would give you the wrong answer. The magi brought valuable gifts, but that was not among them. This dark assertion will be illuminated later on.

Jim drew a package from his overcoat pocket and threw it upon the table.

"Don't make any mistake, Dell," he said, "about me. I don't think there's anything in the way of a haircut or a shave or a shampoo that could make me like my girl any less. But if you'll unwrap that package you may see why you had me going a while at first."

White fingers and nimble tore at the string and paper. And then an ecstatic scream of joy; and then, alas! a quick feminine change to hysterical tears and wails, necessitating the immediate employment of all the comforting powers of the lord of the flat.

For there lay The Combs--the set of combs, side and back, that Della had worshipped long in a Broadway window. Beautiful combs, pure tortoise shell, with jewelled rims--just the shade to wear in the beautiful vanished hair. They were expensive combs, she knew, and her heart had simply craved and yearned over them without the least hope of possession. And now, they were hers, but the tresses that should have adorned the coveted adornments were gone.

But she hugged them to her bosom, and at length she was able to look up with dim eyes and a smile and say: "My hair grows so fast, Jim!" And then Della leaped up like a little singed cat and cried, "Oh, oh!"

Jim had not yet seen his beautiful present. She held it out to him eagerly upon her open palm. The dull precious metal seemed to flash with a reflection of her bright and ardent spirit.

"Isn't it a dandy, Jim? I hunted all over town to find it. You'll have to look at the time a hundred times a day now. Give me your watch. I want to see how it looks on it."

Instead of obeying, Jim tumbled down on the couch and

put his hands under the back of his head and smiled.

"Dell," said he, "let's put our Christmas presents away and keep 'em a while. They're too nice to use just at present. I sold the watch to get the money to buy your combs. And now suppose you put the chops on."

The magi, as you know, were wise men--wonderfully wise men--who brought gifts to the Babe in the manger. They invented the art of giving Christmas presents. Being wise, their gifts were no doubt wise ones, possibly bearing the privilege of exchange in case of duplication. And here I have lamely related to you the uneventful chronicle of two foolish children in a flat who most unwisely sacrificed for each other the greatest treasures of their house. But in a last word to the wise of these days let it be said that of all who give gifts these two were the wisest. O, all who give and receive gifts, such as they are wisest. Everywhere they are wisest. They are the magi.

Day 2 2 Objectives

*Read "The Gift of the Magi" again and *write down in order *all the elements* of a short story listed on Day 1. It is okay if you need some help from your teacher with this exercise.
(See the Answer Key to verify the student's work.) For extra practice in understanding these elements, think about a familiar fairy tale such as "Cinderella" or "Little Red Riding Hood" and identify all of these elements in each one.

Day 3 3 Objectives

*Decide what you would like to write a short story about. You may choose to use your description of your character from Unit 3 in your short story. *Begin to develop* your story around this character by planning your *characters, setting*, and *theme* today. *Write these down.

Day 4 5 Objectives

*Write down the *plot* of your short story, including your *problem, climax,* and *resolution*. Also, *write down your *point of view* and *tone* of your story. *Decide on how much *dialogue* you will include *and who will speak in the dialogue. You may want to use your dialogue from Unit 4 if it can fit into your story.

Day 5 6 Objectives

*Today, find another short story by a well-known author in a book that you have or from the library. It can even be a fairy tale. *Pay close attention to how the author describes his characters and setting. Also, *look at how he develops his theme and plot *and presents his climax. *Take dictation from this short story or the passage from Day 1. *Correct your dictation by comparing it to the book or passage.

Day 6 2 Objectives

Start writing your short story today by focusing on *introducing and *describing your *setting* and your *main character* **only**. This can be done in one or two paragraphs.

Day 7 2 Objectives

*Continue to write your short story. You need to <u>develop</u> your *plot* by presenting the *conflict* or *problem,* working up to the *climax* or *turning point,* and giving your *resolution.* *Make sure your *theme* is <u>clear</u> to your readers.

Day 8 2 Objectives

*Continue writing by <u>developing</u> <u>dialogue</u> between <u>characters</u> and using *specific* **nouns** and *descriptive* **verbs, adjectives,** and **adverbs** throughout your story. *Finish writing your story today.

Day 9 4 Objectives

*Have your teacher or another student read your short story out loud to you. *Make sure you have included <u>all</u> of the *important elements* of a short story. *Proofread your story using the "Proofreading Checklist". *Make all necessary corrections.

Day 10 1 Objective

*Rewrite or type your story and place it in your writing portfolio.

www.edudps.com

UNIT 6
WRITING A FABLE

Day 1 6 Objectives (each objective is indicated by an asterisk)

*Look up the word *fable* in your dictionary. *Write down or read this definition out loud until you <u>understand</u> it. <u>Make</u> <u>sure</u> that you know what a fable is.
*Read these two fables by Aesop.

"The Ants and the Grasshopper"

THE ANTS were spending a fine winter's day drying grain collected in the summertime. A Grasshopper, perishing with famine, passed by and earnestly begged for a little food. The Ants inquired of him, "Why did you not treasure up food during the summer?" He replied, "I had not leisure enough. I passed the days in singing." They then said in derision: "If you were foolish enough to sing all the summer, you must dance supperless to bed in the winter."

"The Shepherd's Boy and the Wolf"

A SHEPHERD-BOY, who watched a flock of sheep near a village, brought out the villagers three or four times by crying out, "Wolf! Wolf!" and when his neighbors came to help him, laughed at them for their pains. The Wolf, however, did truly come at last. The Shepherd-boy, now really alarmed, shouted in an agony of terror: "Pray, do come and help me; the Wolf is killing the sheep"; but no one paid any heed to his cries, nor rendered any assistance. The Wolf, having no cause of fear, at his leisure lacerated or destroyed the whole flock.

*What is the same about these two fables?
*What is different?
*What moral lessons is Aesop trying to teach through the fables?

Day 2 9 Objectives

*Read "How To Write A Fable" in the "How to Write Guide" for the necessary elements needed in a fable. *Read the two fables by Aesop again. *Have your teacher read the fables out loud while you close your eyes. *What do you "see"? What do you "hear"?* *Underline all descriptive **verbs** in green, **adjectives** in red, and **adverbs** in blue that Aesop used. *Circle all *specific* **nouns**.
(See the Answer Key to verify the student's work.) *Did Aesop use *dialogue* in either fable to help his readers understand his *characters*? *What did the animals say? *What animals did Aesop use and *why do you think he picked these particular animals?

Day 3 5 Objectives

Aesop is not the only fable writer, but he is the best known. *Find another fable by Aesop or another writer in a book in your house or from the library. *Write down the *similar characteristics* that you see between the two fables from Day 1 and this new fable. *Write down the *moral lesson* of this fable. *Take dictation from your teacher from either this new fable or one of the other ones from Day 1. *Correct your dictation by comparing it to the book or passage.

Day 4 2 Objectives

Fables usually have no more than three to four characters. Moral lessons serve as themes in fables. *Decide what *moral lesson* you want to teach through your fable and the *animal characters* you want to use to do this. *Write both of these down.

Day 5 2 Objectives

*Write down two sentences to describe *each of your characters*. Make sure you use *specific* **nouns** and *descriptive* **verbs**, **adjectives**, and **adverbs**. *Write down one sentence to describe your *setting* – the time and place of your fable.
Again, make sure that you use *descriptive* **verbs**, **adjectives**, and **adverbs** and *specific* **nouns**.

Day 6 2 Objectives

*Write down the *plot* of your fable – the events that will take place. *Write down your *problem* and *climax* or *turning point*.

Day 7 2 Objectives

*Decide how you will use *dialogue* to tell your story and introduce your characters. *Write this dialogue *between your characters* using everything you have learned about dialogue so far.
See Unit 4 or the "How To Write Guide" for information on writing dialogues.

Day 8 4 Objectives

*Today, write your fable using all the work you have done in the previous days. *Make sure your readers can understand the *moral lesson* you are trying to teach and *make sure that your writing is both descriptive and vivid.
*After completing your fable, list all of the similarities between your fable and one of Aesop's from Day 1. Make a point by point comparison, naming everything you have learned. (For example – Aesop's moral lesson is _____. My moral lesson is _____. Aesop uses these descriptive words about his characters: _____, _____, _____, etc. I use these words to describe my characters: _____, _____, _____, etc. Look in the "How To Write Guide" under "How To Write A Fable" for the elements of a fable if you cannot remember them.)

Day 9 3 Objectives

*Have your teacher read your fable out loud to you. *Listen for *descriptive* language, the moral of the fable and all the other elements that should be in a fable. *Proofread your fable for these elements and for capitalization, punctuation, spelling, and complete sentences.

Day 10 1 Objective

*Rewrite or type your fable making any needed additions and corrections and place it in your portfolio.

www.edudps.com

UNIT 7
WRITING A FRIENDLY LETTER

Day 1 4 Objectives (each objective is indicated by an asterisk)

*Read this friendly letter from <u>Treasure Island</u> by Robert Louis Stevenson.

> Old Anchor Inn
> Bristol
> March 1, 17--

Dear Livesey,

   As I do not know whether you are at the hall or still in London, I send this in double to both places.

   The ship is bought and fitted. She lies at anchor, ready for sea. You never imagined a sweeter schooner--a child might sail her--two hundred tons; name, HISPANIOLA.

   I got her through my old friend, Blandly, who has proved himself throughout the most surprising trump. The admirable fellow literally slaved in my interest, and so, I may say, did everyone in Bristol, as soon as they got wind of the port we sailed for--treasure, I mean.

   Blandly himself found the HISPANIOLA, and

Diagnostic Prescriptive Services

by the most admirable management got her for the merest trifle. There is a class of men in Bristol monstrously prejudiced against Blandly. They go the length of declaring that this honest creature would do anything for money, that the HISPANIOLA belonged to him, and that he sold it me absurdly high--the most transparent calumnies. None of them dare, however, to deny the merits of the ship.

So far there was not a hitch. The workpeople, to be sure--riggers and what not--were most annoyingly slow, but time cured that. It was the crew that troubled me.

I wished a round score of men--in case of natives, buccaneers, or the odious French--and I had the worry of the deuce itself to find so much as half a dozen, till the most remarkable stroke of fortune brought me the very man that I required.

I was standing on the dock, when, by the merest accident, I fell in talk with him. I found he was an old sailor, kept a public-house, knew all the seafaring men in Bristol, had lost his health ashore, and wanted a good berth as cook to get to sea again. He had hobbled down there that morning, he said, to get a smell of the salt.

I was monstrously touched--so would you have

been--and, out of pure pity, I engaged him on the spot to be ship's cook. Long John Silver, he is called, and has lost a leg, but that I regarded as a recommendation, since he lost it in his country's service, under the immortal Hawke. He has no pension, Livesey. Imagine the abominable age we live in!

Well, sir, I thought I had only found a cook, but it was a crew I had discovered. Between Silver and myself, we got together in a few days a company of the toughest old salts imaginable--not pretty to look at, but fellows, by their faces, of the most indomitable spirit. I declare we could fight a frigate.

Long John even got rid of two out of the six or seven I had already engaged. He showed me in a moment that they were just the sort of fresh-water swabs we had to fear in an adventure of importance.

I am in the most magnificent health and spirits, eating like a bull, sleeping like a tree, yet I shall not enjoy a moment till I hear my old tarpaulins tramping round the capstan. Seaward, ho! Hang the treasure! It's the glory of the sea that has turned my head. So now, Livesey, come post; do not lose an hour, if you respect me.

> Let young Hawkins go at once to see his mother, with Redruth for a guard, and then both come full speed to Bristol.
>
> Sincerely,
John Trelawney

*What is the *purpose* of this letter?
*<u>Where</u> in the letter is this purpose told? *What makes this letter <u>interesting</u>? Write down <u>everything</u> you can think of.

Day 2   7 Objectives

*Read again the friendly letter from Day 1. *<u>Underline</u> all *descriptive language*. *Circle all *specific nouns*. *Put brackets [ ] around the sentence or sentences where the *purpose* of the letter is stated.
(See the Answer Key to verify the student's work.)
*Think of the best letter that you have ever received, written, or read. What elements made it such a good letter? Why, especially, do you think that you can still remember it? What stands out about it? *Think of the features of friendly letters that you like to receive from people. *Write these features down.

Day 3   3 Objectives

*Study the friendly letter form on page 91 in the "How To Write Guide" in the back of this book.
*Decide on a person that you would like to write a friendly letter to and the purpose of your letter. You need at least *one main purpose*. *Read "How To Write A Friendly Letter" in the "How To Write Guide".

Day 4 5 Objectives

*Find a letter in a book you have at home or a letter that someone has written. Your parents may even have some very old, well-written letters from relatives, etc.
*Does this letter have an *introduction*, *main paragraph*, and *conclusion*?
*What makes this letter interesting? Write these items down.
*Have your teacher give you a *descriptive sentence* for dictation either from this letter or the letter from Day 1. *Correct your dictation by comparing it to the letter you found or the passage.

Day 5 3 Objectives

*Write the *introductory paragraph* of your letter. *Remember that this paragraph should include *well wishes* to the person you are writing to and perhaps *comments* about the last time that you saw or heard from this person or *comments* about a letter you received from him. *This paragraph should also state the *purpose* of your letter.

Day 6 2 Objectives

*Write the *main paragraph* of your letter, which contains your *purpose* for writing. *Remember that your main paragraph must <u>begin</u> with a <u>topic sentence</u> and <u>end</u> with a <u>concluding sentence</u>. Your purpose could be to tell a story about something special that just happened or to give an invitation to something special that will take place in the future.

Day 7 1 Objective

*Write your *concluding paragraph*. See "How To Write A Friendly Letter" in the "How To Write Guide" for details.

Day 8 1 Objective

*Put your entire letter together, *making sure* that you follow the correct *form* for a friendly letter.

Day 9 4 Objectives

*Have someone read your letter out loud to you. *<u>Make</u> <u>sure</u> the *purpose* of your letter is *clear* and that you have used *descriptive* **verbs**, **adjectives**, and **adverbs** and that some of your **nouns** are *specific*.
*Is your letter interesting?
*Proofread your letter for *descriptive* language, *specific* nouns, <u>punctuation</u>, <u>capitalization</u>, <u>spelling</u> <u>errors</u>, and <u>form</u>.

Day 10 2 Objectives

*Rewrite or type your letter. *Place it in your portfolio.

UNIT 8
WRITING POETRY – RHYMING VERSE

Day 1   4 Objectives (each objective is indicated by an asterisk)

*Read the poem "The Daffodils" by William Wordsworth.

> I wandered lonely as a cloud
>   That floats on high o'er vales and hills,
> When all at once I saw a crowd, --
>   A host of golden daffodils
> Beside the lake, beneath the trees,
> Fluttering and dancing in the breeze.
>
> Continuous as the stars that shine
>   And twinkle on the Milky Way,
> They stretched in never-ending line
>   Along the margin of a bay:
> Ten thousand saw I, at a glance,
> Tossing their heads in sprightly dance.

> The waves beside them danced, but they
> > Outdid the sparkling waves in glee;
> A poet could not but be gay
> > In such a jocund company;
> I gazed – and gazed – but little thought
> What wealth the show to me had brought.
>
> For oft, when on my couch I lie,
> > In vacant or in pensive mood,
> They flash upon that inward eye
> > Which is the bliss of solitude;
> And then my heart with pleasure fills,
> And dances with the daffodils.

*Close your eyes and have your teacher read this poem out loud to you. What do you *see*?

Memorize these definitions and *discuss* them with your teacher.
- Poetry: language that shows imagination, emotion, and thinking in verse form.
- Figure of Speech: a form of expression used to convey meaning by comparing or identifying one thing with another.
- Rhyme Scheme: the pattern of rhyme used in a poem, usually marked by letters to show the pattern. For example, in the poem:
  > Roses are red, a
  > Violets are blue, b

Sugar is sweet, c

And so are you. b

The rhyme scheme is: a b c b.

- Stanza: a division of a poem consisting of a series of lines arranged together in a recurring pattern.

Day 2   6 Objectives

*Underline all *descriptive* **verbs** in green, **adjectives** in red, and **adverbs** in blue that you can find in the poem from Day 1. *Circle all *specific* **nouns**.

(See the Answer Key to verify the student's work.)

(Review the meanings of these parts of speech if you need to.)

*Make a list of all the **verbs** this poet used *to describe* the daffodils.

*Define any unfamiliar words, such as jocund, pensive, bliss, or solitude.

*Look for the words that *rhyme* in this poem. *Using different colors, underline the words that *rhyme*, with each rhyming sound having its own color.

Day 3   2 Objectives

*Memorize and then *discuss the meanings of the following figures of speech with your teacher.

> Imagery: the words a poet uses to bring forth *images* or *pictures in the mind* of the reader.
>
> Simile: the *comparison* of two *unlike* objects using the words "*like*" or "*as*". Example: "My love is *like* a red, red rose".
>
> Personification: a *figure of speech* in which an *animal*, *object*, or *idea* takes on *characteristics of a person*. Example: "The rain *danced* on the street."

Day 4 3 Objectives

*Review the definitions from yesterday, and *answer these questions:
<u>What</u> does the poet *compare himself to* in the first line?
<u>What</u> does the poet *compare the daffodils to* in the first line of the second stanza?
<u>What</u> are these *comparisons* called?
*Write down examples of <u>personification</u> from each stanza.

Day 5 5 Objectives

*Find a rhyming poem by a well-known author in a book that you have.
*List all <u>figures of speech</u> and *the *rhyme scheme.*
*Get your teacher to give you dictation from the poem or from "The Daffodils".
*Correct your dictation by comparing it to the book or passage.

Day 6 4 Objectives

*Choose a *subject*, other than a person, to write your poem about. Think of something that you have closely observed or already know a lot about. This can be an *object, place, period of time,* or *event*. Make a list of *specific* **nouns** for your poem.
*Write down as many *descriptive words* that you can think of to describe your subject. Use **verbs**, **adjectives**, and **adverbs**.
*Think of some *objects to compare* your subject *with*. *Write these down as <u>similes</u>.

Day 7 4 Objectives

*Think of some ways your subject can *show human qualities.* *Write these down as examples of personification to use in your poem. *Decide on your *rhyme scheme* for your poem. (You may want to use the same rhyme scheme as "The Daffodils" so that you will have a model to follow.) *Write down the words that you will use to rhyme.

Day 8 6 Objectives

*Compare your *descriptive* **verbs**, **adjectives**, and **adverbs** with William Wordsworth's that you underlined on Day 2. *Compare your figures of speech with Mr. Wordsworth's. *Use your thesaurus and write down other words that could be substituted for these descriptions and figures of speech. *Write your poem today. Use all *descriptive language* and *figures of speech that you have decided on.

Day 9 4 Objectives

*Have someone read your poem out loud to you. *Make sure that you hear *rhyme* *and can virtually see, *hear, feel, smell* or *taste* because of the *descriptive language* you have used.
*Proofread your poem for correct punctuation, capitalization, and spelling.

Day 10 2 Objectives

*Rewrite or type your poem. You may also choose to illustrate your poem with a picture or painting.
*Place your poem in your portfolio.

UNIT 9

WRITING POETRY – A BALLAD OR NARRATIVE POEM

Day 1   2 Objectives (each objective is indicated by an asterisk)

*Memorize this definition for ballad.

Ballad: *A poem that tells a story and is designed to be put to music or recited out loud. It may or may not rhyme, but it usually does.*

Since a ballad is a story written as a poem, it will have many or most of the elements of a short story.

*Read "Paul Revere's Ride" by Henry Wadsworth Longfellow.

> Listen, my children, and you shall hear
> Of the midnight ride of Paul Revere,
> On the eighteenth of April, in Seventy-five;
> Hardly a man is now alive
> Who remembers that famous day and year.
>
> He said to his friend, "If the British march
> By land or sea from the town to-night,
> Hang a lantern aloft in the belfry arch
> Of the North Church tower as a signal light,--
> One, if by land, and two, if by sea;
> And I on the opposite shore will be,
> Ready to ride and spread the alarm
> Through every Middlesex village and farm
> For the country folk to be up and to arm,"

Then he said, "Good night!" and with muffled oar
Silently rowed to the Charlestown shore,
Just as the moon rose over the bay,
Where swinging wide at her moorings lay
The Somerset, British man-of-war;
A phantom ship, with each mast and spar
Across the moon like a prison bar,
And a huge black hulk, that was magnified
By its own reflection in the tide.

Meanwhile, his friend, through alley and street,
Wanders and watches with eager ears,
Till in the silence around him he hears
The muster of men at the barrack door,
The sound of arms, and the tramp of feet,
And the measured tread of the grenadiers,
Marching down to their boats on the shore.

Then he climbed the tower of the Old North Church,
By the wooden stairs, with stealthy tread,
To the belfry-chamber overhead,
And startled the pigeons from their perch
On the sombre rafters, that round him made
Masses and moving shapes of shade,--
By the trembling ladder, steep and tall
To the highest window in the wall,

Where he paused to listen and look down
A moment on the roofs of the town,
And the moonlight flowing over all.

Beneath, in the churchyard, lay the dead,
In their night-encampment on the hill,
Wrapped in silence so deep and still
That he could hear, like a sentinel's tread,
The watchful night-wind, as it went
Creeping along from tent to tent
And seeming to whisper, "All is well!"
A moment only he feels the spell
Of the place and the hour, and the secret dread
Of the lonely belfry and the dead;
For suddenly all his thoughts are bent
On a shadowy something far away,
Where the river widens to meet the bay,--
A line of black that bends and floats
On the rising tide, like a bridge of boats.

Meanwhile, impatient to mount and ride,
Booted and spurred, with a heavy stride
On the opposite shore walked Paul Revere.
Now he patted his horse's side,
Now gazed at the landscape far and near,
Then, impetuous, stamped the earth,

And turned and tightened his saddle-girth;
But mostly he watched with eager search
The belfry-tower of the Old North Church,
As it rose above the graves on the hill,
Lonely and spectral and sombre and still.
And lo! as he looks, on the belfry's height
A glimmer, and then a gleam of light!
He springs to the saddle, the bridle he turns,
But lingers and gazes, till full on his sight
A second lamp in the belfry burns!

A hurry of hoofs in a village street,
A shape in the moonlight, a bulk in the dark,
And beneath, from the pebbles, in passing, a spark
Struck out by a steed flying fearless and fleet:
That was all! And yet, through the gloom and the light,
The fate of a nation was riding that night;
And the spark struck out by that steed, in his flight,
Kindled the land into flame with its heat.
He has left the village and mounted the steep,
And beneath him, tranquil and broad and deep,
Is the Mystic, meeting the ocean tides;
And under the alders, that skirt its edge,
Now soft on the sand, now loud on the ledge,
Is heard the tramp of his steed as he rides.

It was twelve by the village clock
When he crossed the bridge into Medford town.
He heard the crowing of the cock,
And the barking of the farmer's dog,
And felt the damp of the river fog,
That rises after the sun goes down.

It was one by the village clock,
When he galloped into Lexington.
He saw the gilded weathercock
Swim in the moonlight as he passed,
And the meeting-house windows, blank and bare,
Gaze at him with a spectral glare,
As if they already stood aghast
At the bloody work they would look upon.

It was two by the village clock,
When he came to the bridge in Concord town.
He heard the bleating of the flock,
And the twitter of birds among the trees,
And felt the breath of the morning breeze
Blowing over the meadows brown.
And one was safe and asleep in his bed
Who at the bridge would be first to fall,
Who that day would be lying dead,
Pierced by a British musket-ball.

You know the rest. In the books you have read,

How the British Regulars fired and fled,--

How the farmers gave them ball for ball,

From behind each fence and farm-yard wall,

Chasing the red-coats down the lane,

Then crossing the fields to emerge again

Under the trees at the turn of the road,

And only pausing to fire and load.

So through the night rode Paul Revere;

And so through the night went his cry of alarm

To every Middlesex village and farm,--

A cry of defiance and not of fear,

A voice in the darkness, a knock at the door,

And a word that shall echo forevermore!

For, borne on the night-wind of the Past,

Through all our history, to the last,

In the hour of darkness and peril and need,

The people will waken and listen to hear

The hurrying hoof-beats of that steed,

And the midnight message of Paul Revere.

Day 2 3 Objectives

*From memory, tell your teacher the definition of a ballad that you learned yesterday.

*Read the ballad from yesterday again, or have your teacher read it out loud to you.

*Answer the following questions.
- What story is this poem telling?
- What facts about the story does the author think are important enough to tell?
- Who is it about?
- What characters are in the story?
- What is the point of view of the ballad? Is it written in the 1st, 2nd, or 3rd person? (See Unit 5 for definitions.)

Day 3 6 Objectives

*Write down the answers to these questions:
- Is the *rhyme scheme* of "Paul Revere's Ride" the same in each stanza?
- What is the *theme* or *message* of this poem?
- What is the *tone* of the poem?

*Underline all *descriptive* words (**verbs** in green, **adjectives** in red, and **adverbs** in blue) in the ballad.

*Circle all *specific* **nouns**.

(See the Answer Key to verify the student's work.)

*Note the author's extensive use of verbs to help tell his story.

*Underline any *figures of speech* used in the ballad.

*Tell the story of "Paul Revere's Ride" in your own words.

Day 4 7 Objectives

*Think about an historical event or family story that you would like to write a ballad about. *Choose a *setting* (a particular time and place) for your ballad. *Decide on the *theme* or *message* of your ballad such as *courage, love, fear,* etc. *Write down the most important parts of your story that you want to tell. *Include a *problem* or *conflict* to be solved. *Decide which *point of view* you will write your ballad in. *Decide on the *tone* of your ballad. (See Unit 5 for a thorough explanation of the elements of a short story.)

Day 5 4 Objectives

*Write down *specific* **nouns** and *descriptive* **adjectives**, **verbs**, and **adverbs** that you will use to describe your event or tell your story. You may also choose to use several vivid verbs to help relate the story that you want to tell. Use your thesaurus so that you will have plenty of these words in order that your ballad will qualify as descriptive and vivid.
*Write down some *figures of speech* to use in your ballad.
*Decide what your *rhyme scheme* will be for your ballad.
*Write down your words that will rhyme.

Day 6 4 Objectives

*Find another ballad by a well-known author, and from everything you have learned, *determine how the poet tells his story. In other words, does he use figures of speech or dialogue, and how does he portray his theme, setting, and characters?
*Take dictation from your teacher from this ballad or "Paul Revere's Ride". *Correct your dictation by comparing it to your selection or the passage.

Day 7 2 Objectives

*Begin writing your ballad. *<u>Make</u> <u>sure</u> that you use *word pictures* to tell your story and that the *theme* of your poem is <u>clear</u>.

Day 8 1 Objective

*Continue to write your ballad today.

Day 9 6 Objectives

*Finish writing your ballad today.
*Have someone read your ballad out loud to you. **Close your eyes* and *see* if you can *visualize* what is being read to you. Could you virtually *hear, smell, taste,* or *feel* things from what was read to you? *<u>Make</u> <u>sure</u> you have a *rhyme scheme* and *that your story is <u>clear</u>.
*Proofread your ballad for <u>punctuation</u>, <u>capitalization</u>, and <u>spelling</u>.

Day 10 2 Objectives

*Rewrite or type your ballad. You may also choose to illustrate your ballad with pictures or illustrations. *Place it in your portfolio.

THREE CHARACTERISTICS THAT MAKE THE BEST WRITING *THE BEST*

The *great works of world literature* and the *classics* have these three main characteristics in common:

1. They are **timeless and enduring**. This means that readers of all time periods enjoy reading them because they deal with *human character traits* – good and bad – that never change and are fascinating. People of all ages and time can relate to or are fascinated by what is written in these writings, so they continue to read them over many years.

   Rule 1: Focus on and develop a variety of character traits – the more varied the better.

2. **The authors paint "word pictures"** in descriptions of places, objects, and characters. In other words, the writing is so descriptive that you can virtually see, hear, feel, taste, or smell what is being described in these writings. All of these things become real to you as you read because the authors have taken great care in how they use words as they write. These authors have selected very *descriptive* and *vivid* verbs, adjectives, and adverbs, with some *specific* nouns, to paint their word pictures.

   Rule 2: Paint your writings with descriptive, vivid, and specific parts of speech throughout.

3. The *subjects* and *themes* of these writings are so **interesting**, **entertaining**, and **exciting** that they have captured the interest of readers over the years. Most of the themes revolve around challenging problems that must be solved by the main characters.

   Rule 3: Captivate your readers with subjects and themes that hold their attention and engage them.

www.edudps.com

PROOFREADING CHECKLIST

Type of genre _____

Put a (√) if present and an (×) if not present. Sometimes not all items will apply to every genre such as dialogues, friendly letters, and poetry.

- ____ The paragraph is indented.
- ____ The paragraph has at least 5 sentences.
- ____ All sentences begin with a capital letter.
- ____ All sentences end with a punctuation mark.
- ____ The paragraph has a good <u>beginning</u> or <u>topic</u> sentence.
- ____ The paragraph has a good <u>ending</u> or <u>concluding</u> sentence.
- ____ All sentences relate to the topic.
- ____ All verbs, adverbs, and adjectives are vivid or descriptive.
- ____ Some nouns are specific rather than generic. For example, "fellow" is used instead of "man".
- ____ All sentences are complete – there are no run-on sentences or fragments.
- ____ All important words (proper nouns) have capital letters.
- ____ The same words are not used too often. For example, words such as "then" or "said".
- ____ The sentences have different lengths. Not all are very short and not all are very long.
- ____ Different kinds of sentences are included – compound, complex, etc.
- ____ Each subject agrees with its verb. For example, improper subject-verb agreement would be: "the dogs barks".
- ____ The same verb tense is used throughout the paper. For example, if you start a story in past tense (what has happened in the past), you must continue with this tense throughout the story.

Diagnostic Prescriptive Services

GRADING CRITERIA

Parents should use this grading system to evaluate their students' writing. Make sure students understand the requirements for grading. Scoring ranges from numbers 5 to 1 with 5 being the highest possible score.

Please note: In rhyming poetry and ballads, only numbers 5, 4, and 1 are required.

5 – All 5 of these important elements are present in the writing:
1. The purpose of the writing is clear and the theme or message is clear.
2. There is a topic sentence at the beginning and a concluding sentence at the end of each paragraph.
3. There are sentences to support the main topic sentence.
4. Vivid or descriptive verbs, adjectives, and adverbs and some specific nouns are used.
5. Sentences are complete with correct punctuation, capitalization, and grammar.

4 – Four of the above are present. (Designate which ones are missing on the paper.)

3 – Three of the above are present. (Designate which ones are missing on the paper.)

2 – Two of the above are present. (Designate which ones are missing on the paper.)

1 – Work is not acceptable. The writing lacks the features of good writing or is not organized and should be redone.

www.edudps.com

LEARNING STYLES SUGGESTIONS
AND OTHER WAYS TO AUGMENT THIS CURRICULUM

Note: When possible, use all the suggestions regarding all learners because this has been proven to help insure retention of the material.

Tactile/Kinesthetic Learners

1. Purchase a large dry-erase board with large red markers for students to use to write their assignments on or to complete other exercises on, such as dictation.
2. To help students understand the literary passages, have them act out the action scenes so that the story comes alive. They may also enjoy and benefit from acting out their own stories.
3. Tactile learners will enjoy drawing pictures to illustrate their writings.
4. Allow these students to type their assignments, if they are able.
5. These learners sometimes have problems with handwriting or putting thoughts on paper, so you may need to do their writing for them as they dictate to you.

Visual Learners

1. Use highlighters and various colors of ink to mark important information in the assignments.
2. These learners will also benefit from proofreading their papers with different colors of ink for different mistakes.

Auditory Learners

1. Auditory learners will enjoy and benefit from narrating (telling the story in their own words) the literary passages back to their teachers.
2. Often it is helpful for these students to first dictate their responses into a tape recorder and then write their assignments from the recording.

General Suggestions

1. Each student should keep a writing portfolio of their final writings with any artistic illustrations they have made to accompany them. Hard-back notebooks (binders) are best for this, but any kind of notebook can be used. This is helpful for students to see the accomplishments and improvements they have made over the school year in their writings.

2. To encourage your students about their writing, I highly recommend that you put on an "Author's Tea" twice a year (around Christmas and in May or June). You can keep this very simple by inviting a few friends and family members and serving simple tea or punch and cookies. Guests are to view all of the "author's" writings and make encouraging comments on comment sheets for the students to keep in their writing portfolios. Students can also read some of their writings out loud to their guests. This is an excellent way to encourage students to write more.

www.edudps.com

ADDITIONAL LITERARY PASSAGES FOR MODELING WRITING

Teachers please note:

One main objective of this curriculum is to teach students to become aware of and to learn to analyze great works of literature. Therefore, as your students progress in the curriculum, they need to start finding additional examples of the writing genres <u>on their own</u>. *The examples listed below are primarily for the teachers to use as they go through the curriculum <u>again</u> with their students in order to continue to reinforce good writing skills. To use these additional passages, simply substitute them for the original passages included at the beginning of each unit and <u>follow the same daily objectives</u>*.

Description of an Object

- <u>Little House in the Big Woods</u> by L. Wilder

    Chapter 4 – description of the rag doll

- <u>The Silver Chair</u> by C. S. Lewis

    Chapter 12 – description of the Serpent Queen

- <u>The Time Machine</u> by H. G. Wells

    Chapter 1 – description of the model of the time machine

- "Theseus and the Minotaur" from <u>Heroes, Gods, and Monsters of the Greek Myths</u> by B. Evslin – description of the minotaur

- <u>Pilgrim's Progress</u> by J. Bunyan – description of Apollyon

- <u>The War of the Worlds</u> by H. G. Wells

    Part 2, Chapter 2 – description of a martian

Description of a Place

- <u>Prince Caspian</u> by C. S. Lewis

    Chapter 1 – description of the island and the beach

Diagnostic Prescriptive Services

- <u>Black Beauty</u> by A. Sewell

    Chapter 4 – description of the park

- <u>Peter Pan</u> by J. M. Barrie

    Chapter 7 – description of the home of the lost boys in Neverland

- <u>To Kill a Mockingbird</u> by H. Lee

    Chapter 1 – description of the town of Maycomb

- <u>Pilgrim's Progress</u> by J. Bunyan – description of Vanity Fair and the Celestial City

- <u>Anne of Green Gables</u> by L. M. Montgomery

    Chapter 4 – description of Green Gables

Description of a Character

- <u>20,000 Leagues Under the Sea</u> by J. Verne

    Chapter 8 – description of a sailor

- <u>Ivanhoe</u> by Sir W. Scott

    Chapter 1 – description of the woodsmen

- <u>The Time Machine</u> by H. G. Wells

    Chapter 2 – description of the time traveler

- <u>A Wonder Book</u> by N. Hawthorne

    Myth 1 – description of the Gorgon sisters

- <u>Old Yeller</u> by F. Gipson

    Chapter 2 – description of Old Yeller, the dog

- <u>Treasure Island</u> by R. L. Stevenson

    Chapter 1 – description of the buccaneer

- <u>The Old Man and the Sea</u> by E. Hemingway

    Chapter 1, first page – description of the man

- <u>Huckleberry Finn</u> by M. Twain

    Chapter 2 – description of Pap

Dialogues

- The Lion, the Witch, and the Wardrobe by C. S. Lewis
  Chapter 2 – the beginning dialogue
- The Prince and the Pauper by M. Twain
  Chapter 3 – dialogue between the Prince and the Pauper
- Charlotte's Web by E. B. White
  Chapter 5 – dialogue between Wilbur and Charlotte
- The Invisible Man by H. G. Wells
  Chapter 9 – all dialogue
- The Hobbit by J. R. R. Tolkien
  Chapter 12 – dialogue between Smaug and Bilbo

Short Stories

- "The Fir Tree" by H. C. Anderson
- "Kidnapped Santa Claus" by L. F. Baum
- Just So Stories by R. Kipling
  (any short story in this book)
- "Jim Baker's Blue-Jay Yarn" by M. Twain
- "The Red-Headed League" from Adventures of Sherlock Holmes by Sir A. C. Doyle
- "Rip Van Winkle" from The Sketch-Book of Geoffrey Crayon, Gent. by W. Irving

Fables

- Any of Aesop's Fables, especially "Androcles and the Lion" and "The Hare and the Tortoise"
- "The Canterbury Tales" by G. Chaucer
  "Chanticleer and Pertelote"
- "The Falcon and the Partridge" from The Arabian Nights by A. Lang
- "Minerva and the Owl" from The Arabian Nights by A. Lang

Friendly Letters

- Little Women by L. M. Alcott

  Chapter 12

- "Letters of Pliny the Younger"

  Letter to Cornelius Tacitus

Poetry that Rhymes

- A Child's Garden of Verses by R. L. Stevenson (entire book of poems)
- "The Singing Children" by M. Twain
- "Good Night" by V. Hugo
- "Duck's Ditty" by K. Grahame
- "The Baby" by C. McDonald
- "The Road Not Taken" by R. Frost
- "The Eagle" by A. Tennyson

Ballads (Narrative Poetry)

- "The Rime of the Ancient Mariner" by S. T. Coleridge
- "Robin Hood and Friar Tuck" – anonymous
- "Lord Ullin's Daughter" by T. Campbell
- "Annabel Lee" by E. A. Poe
- "The Charge of the Light Brigade" by A. Tennyson

www.edudps.com

HOW TO WRITE GUIDE

Note: The following facts apply in writing:
- Titles of books are always underlined or italicized.
- Chapter headings in books are always given in quotation marks.
- Titles of short stories are always given in quotation marks.
- Titles of poems, both rhyming and narrative, are always given in quotation marks.

Use your thesaurus to enrich your vocabulary of descriptive and specific language for all of the following genres.

HOW TO WRITE A DESCRIPTIVE PARAGRAPH

1. Choose either an object, place, or character that you wish to describe in a paragraph. The description of a character can be either a person or an animal.
2. When choosing an object, observe or consider it closely for details to describe. This may include color, size and shape. Compare your object to other objects in order to help describe it.
3. When describing a place, pick a place that is familiar to you or that interests you. Observe this place by looking at it in person or in books. Think about the people, events, and specific feelings that may make this place different. Think about the physical characteristics of this place, its people, and their actions that can effectively show what the place looks like and what kind of a place it is. Compare your place to other places in order to help describe it.
4. When describing a person, think about the characteristics that make this character different from others. Describe the character's behavior, appearance, and actions, including goals, attitudes, concerns, hob-

bies, etc. Use events or actions to show what your character is like. Compare your character to other people in order to help describe him.

5. Use as many descriptive or vivid adjectives, verbs, and adverbs that you can think of to describe your object, place, or character. Use some specific nouns throughout your description instead of only using generic nouns. In describing a character, remember to describe the character's behavior, appearance, and actions.

6. Your paragraph must have a topic sentence. Remember that your topic sentence should tell what your entire paragraph will be about. However, don't <u>ever</u> write a topic sentence that says: "I am going to describe _____".

7. Your paragraph must have support sentences that describe your topic. An adequate paragraph must have at least 5 sentences, with at least 3 of them being support sentences. Remember that you are painting "word pictures" of your topic so that people will be able to virtually see, hear, feel, taste or smell what you are describing.

8. Your paragraph must have a concluding sentence that mainly restates your topic sentence, but in different words.

HOW TO WRITE A DIALOGUE

1. Dialogue is conversation involving two or more characters. Come up with the characters that will speak in your dialogue. If you are including your dialogue in a short story, you have already developed at least your main character, setting, and theme for your story.

2. Decide how your characters will speak. Will they use Standard English or will they speak in a certain dialect?

3. Decide what you want to say about your characters, your theme, and your story through this dialogue. Come up with your introductory and concluding sentences that come before and after the actual quotations. These sentences should also be descriptive.

4. Remember that quotation marks go outside the ending punctuation marks. For example: "What did you say, Ted?" "I will not do it!"

5. Remember that commas go inside the quotation marks when someone speaks, before telling who spoke. For example: "Well, it isn't," replied the friend kindly. However, you do not include commas when the ending punctuation is a ? or !.

   For example: "What did you say, Ted?" inquired Bill.

6. Do not follow the same pattern each time someone speaks, such as "_ _ _," he **said** or "_ _ _," she **said**. Use the word "said" as little as possible. Come up with descriptive verbs instead of the word "said". Try using "mumbled", "blurted", "replied", "added", etc.

7. Break up the sentence and put the character speaking in the middle sometimes. This is called a split quotation. For example: "However," he mumbled, "we will find you."

8. Use vivid language in your dialogue to tell how your characters are speaking. For example: "I will not view such a disgusting sight," Susan *bellowed angrily.*

9. Each time a new person speaks, start a new paragraph. Never have two or more characters speaking inside of a single paragraph.

HOW TO WRITE A SHORT STORY

(For a thorough explanation and definition of all the elements of a short story, see Unit 5, Day 1.)

1. Decide on a subject, time period, or theme you would like to write about.
2. Develop your plot (what will happen in your story). (a) Decide what the conflict or problem of your story will be. (b) Determine what main events will happen in your story. Remember that a short story is short, so make sure you don't have too many characters or too many things happening. (c) Determine your climax or turning point of the action. (d) Decide on your resolution – how your problem will be solved.
3. Determine your main character or characters and minor characters also. Think about the personalities you want your characters to have or the way you want them to act. Use vivid adjectives to describe each character.
4. Determine your setting for your story – the time and place of your story. This should be introduced at the beginning of your story.
5. Develop your theme – the message of your story or what lesson you want to teach your reader. This should be clear throughout your short story.
6. Determine your narrator or which point of view you will write in. See Unit 5, Day 1 for more detail.
7. Decide on the tone of your story. Will it be serious, funny, sarcastic, angry, etc.?
8. When writing your short story, introduce your setting and characters first. Use dialogue to present or show your characters to your readers. See "How To Write A Dialogue" in this guide. Use descriptive language when describing your characters and setting. See Unit 2 and Unit 3 on how to write these descriptions.

9. Make sure that the problem in your story and the way that it is solved are both clear. Also, make sure that your climax or turning point is clear to your readers.

HOW TO WRITE A FABLE

1. Decide what moral lesson you would like to teach through your fable.
2. Choose your characters. Usually these characters are animals, and each fable should contain no more than three or four characters. Use descriptive language to introduce and describe your characters.
3. Decide on your setting – the time and place of your story.
4. Develop your plot or the events that will happen. Arrange these events to interest or excite your readers. Make sure you have a climax or turning point in your fable.
5. Decide whether you will use dialogue between your characters. Dialogue between characters often makes a story more interesting; however, not all fables use dialogue.
6. If using dialogue, determine what your dialogue will be and use it to show who your characters are, facts about their personalities, or the way they act. Use descriptive language when writing your dialogue.
7. Finally, when writing your fable, bring all the previous points together.

HOW TO WRITE A FRIENDLY LETTER

1. Decide both whom you will write your letter to and the purpose of your letter. You must have at least one main purpose such as: (a) telling about something important that has happened or something that will happen (b) inviting someone to an important event or (c) asking the person that you are writing to about his health or other important things in his life.

2. Make sure that you precisely follow the correct form for your friendly letter. (See the form on the next page.)

3. Your letter must have an <u>introductory</u> paragraph. It does not have to be long. Your introductory paragraph should include (a) an expression of good wishes and perhaps comments about the last time that you saw the person or a letter that you last received from him and (b) a topic sentence to tell the purpose of your letter.

4. Your letter must have a <u>main</u> paragraph that contains your main purpose for writing. This paragraph must also include a topic sentence and a concluding sentence. This paragraph can be a story about an event that just took place. You can even use dialogue to make it more interesting. It can be an invitation to an important event in which you give the time, place, and date of the event and a description of what will take place. *This paragraph should be as descriptive and interesting as possible.* Make sure that you use descriptive verbs, adjectives, and adverbs.

5. Aside from the one paragraph that contains your main purpose for writing, you may also want to add additional paragraphs.

6. Your letter must contain a concluding paragraph. It does not have to be long. Your concluding paragraph should express kindness or affection to the person you are writing to and contain any questions you would like this person to answer in his next letter.

www.edudps.com

Heading: Name
                                            Address
                                            Date

Greeting: Dear _____,

Introductory   _____
Paragraph: _____
                 _____
                 _____
                 _____

Main Para-   _____
graph with   _____
purpose: _____
                 _____
                 _____

Concluding   _____
Paragraph: _____
                 _____
                 _____
                 _____

Closing: Your friend,
                                            Dale

HOW TO WRITE RHYMING VERSE

1. Choose a subject for your poem. This can be an object, a place, a period of time, a person, or an event. It will be easier if you choose something you have observed very closely or already have knowledge about.
2. Use as many descriptive words that you can think of to describe your subject. Use verbs, adjectives, and adverbs.
3. Think of some other objects to compare your subject with. (See Unit 8 for definitions of figures of speech.) Use imagery and similes.
4. Think of some ways that your subject can show human qualities. (See definitions for personification in Unit 8.) Use examples of personification in your poem.
5. Decide on the rhyme scheme of your poem or which lines and words will rhyme.
6. After writing your poem, read it out loud to make sure you have used descriptive language that creates pictures in the minds of your readers.

HOW TO WRITE A BALLAD OR NARRATIVE POEM

(Review all the elements of a short story from Unit 5 before writing your ballad.)

1. Choose an historical event or family story that you would like to write a ballad about.
2. Decide on a setting (a particular time and place) for your ballad.
3. Decide on which point of view you will write from.
4. Determine the most important parts of this historical event or family story. Make sure that you include a conflict or problem.
5. Choose a theme or message, such as *love, faith, courage,* or *fear* that you want your ballad to tell.
6. Use descriptive adjectives, adverbs, and verbs to describe your event or tell your story.
7. Use some specific nouns rather than using all generic ones.
8. Use some figures of speech in your ballad. (See Unit 8 for definitions.)
9. Decide on your rhyme scheme for your ballad. Choose words that will rhyme in your ballad.
10. When writing your ballad, make sure that your story and theme are clear and that you paint word pictures through descriptive and vivid language.

ANSWER KEY TO CITED LITERARY PASSAGES

Note: Not all nouns, verbs, adjectives, and adverbs in each literary passage are listed in this answer key – only the most descriptive ones that the author uses to create word pictures for the readers.

Adjectives in the form of "of ___" are prepositional phrases used as adjectives.

Remember that younger and inexperienced students should not be expected to find every example.

- All entries in the answer key are placed in alphabetical order under each particular part of speech.
- We have not changed the spelling of the parts of speech listed. We have reproduced the spelling as rendered by each author.

20,000 Leagues Under the Sea

Specific Nouns (circle)	Descriptive Verbs (green)	Descriptive Adjectives (red)	Descriptive Adverbs (blue)
beak	brought	air	carefully
cephalopods	changing	eight	crossways
chance	figure	enormous	out
Creature	fixed	fleshly	successively
cuttlefish	furnished	formidable	vertically
freak	inspired	great	
furies' hair	irritated	green	
gesture	lose	horned	
hearts	opened	horrible	
holes	overcame	immense	
horror	passed	inner	
irritation	possess	livid grey	

nouns (circle)	verbs (green)	adjectives (red)
jaws	quivering	marvellous
mass	repress	of disgust
mollusc	shut	of shears
monsters	studying	pointed
movements	swam	reddish brown
Nautilus	taking	several
opportunity	twisted	spindle-like
pair	watching	staring
poulps	weigh	three
presence	wish	varying
rows		veritable
shears		worthy
side		
specimen		
substance		
suckers		
tentacles		
vigour		
vitality		

A Christmas Carol

Specific Nouns (circle)	Descriptive Verbs (green)	Descriptive Adjectives (red)	Descriptive Adverbs (blue)
berries	beating	ancient	about
blaze	brewing	biting	afterwards
brazier	chattering	bleak	already
breasts	come	brown	always
brightness	conduct	city	busy

Diagnostic Prescriptive Services

nouns (circle)	verbs (green)	adjectives (red)	adverbs (blue)
candles	crackled	cold	down
chink	drooping	congealed	hard by
cloud	flaring	dark	meanwhile
corner	gathered	dense	outside
counting-house	lighted	dingy	quite
court	obscuring	every	round
darkness	passed	flaring	slily
feet	peeping	foggy	so
fog	pouring	frozen	sullenly
head	proffering	good	up
ice	ran	Gothic	up there
keyhole	repairing	great	withal
labourers	sat	gruff	without
links	stamping	holly	
Nature	struck	intense	
offices	thickened	invisible	
overflowing	turned	large	
party	warm	light	
phantoms	warming	main	
rapture	wheezing	mere	
scale	winking	misanthropic	
services		narrowest	
smears		neighbouring	
solitude		old	
sprigs		opposite	
stones		pale	
vibrations		palpable	
waterplug		pavement	
weather		ragged	

adjectives (red)

ruddy

tremalous

Robinson Crusoe

Specific Nouns (circle)	Descriptive Verbs (green)	Descriptive Adjectives (red)	Descriptive Adverbs (blue)
America	awoke	agreeable	again
aspect	beckoned	antic	down
Brazilians	complied	black	flat
cake	describe	bright	likewise
cave	espied	close	perfectly
countenance	kept	comely	quickly
disposition	laid	curled	quite
European	laying	dun-olive	stark
face	lived	earthen	too
fellow	made	fierce	very
forehead	milking	fine	well
Friday	pleased	glad	
gestures	reckon	good	
inclosure	running	great	
ivory	saved	handsome	
limbs	serve	high	
Master	set	humble	
memory	slept	large	
natives	slumbered	little	
servitude	smiled	long	
sharpness	sop	manly	
signs	speak	naked	

Diagnostic Prescriptive Services

nouns (circle)	verbs (green)	adjectives (red)
softness	taught	plump
subjection	teach	round
submission		small
sweetness		sparkling
Virginians		straight
vivacity		strong
wool		surly
		tall
		tawny
		thankful
		thin
		twenty-six
		well-shaped
		white

The Wind in the Willows

Specific Nouns (circle)	Descriptive Verbs (green)	Descriptive Adjectives (red)	Descriptive Adverbs (blue)
animal-etiquette	accounts	active	actually
embers	assented	arduous	at last
energy	basking	awful	back
fire	care	bad	bad
firelight	chatted	decent	decently
force	cocked	full	fidgety
fragments	continued	glowing	full
hang	convinced	good	gloomily
law	employ	great	gravely
millionaire	feels	hard	heartily

nouns (circle)	verbs (green)	adjectives (red)	adverbs (blue)
muscle	felt	heaven-born	hopelessly
nonsense	finished	heroic	
off-season	gathered	higher	independent
order	going	incapable	last
reason	inquired	jolly	late
settle	insist	old	less
skin	killed	regardless	literally
smash-up	leave	rich	moderately
stretch	look	safe	more
sunrise	make	sensible	mournful
trouble	nodded	shorter	now
	piled	sleepy	only
	put	steady	properly
	resting	strenuous	quite
	rouses	tight	rather
	ruined	weather-bound	really
	stand	well-trained	round
	tested	wood	seriously
	turned		severely
	understanding		simply
			so
			up
			worse

"The Gift of the Magi"

1. <u>Main characters</u>: Jim and Della Young
2. <u>Setting</u>: Christmas (in an apartment mainly and a store)
3. <u>Theme</u>: the sacrifice of giving, love
4. <u>Plot</u>: <u>Conflict</u> – How to buy (or afford) a Christmas present for her (Della's) husband

Diagnostic Prescriptive Services

Resolution – Della sells her hair to get money to buy Jim a present.

Climax – Della and Jim discover that each one has sacrificed her and his most important possession to buy a gift for each other.

5. <u>Point of View</u>: third person
6. <u>Dialogue</u>: There are dialogues between Madame and Della and Jim and Della that help tell the story.
7. <u>Tone</u>: Serious

"The Ants and the Grasshopper"

Moral: Preparing for the days of necessity has reward, while ill-advised leisure brings loss.

Specific Nouns (circle)	**Descriptive Verbs** (green)	**Descriptive Adjectives** (red)	**Descriptive Adverbs** (blue)
bed	begged	fine	by
derision	collected	foolish	earnestly
famine	dance	little	enough
food	drying	winter's	supperless
grain	inquired		
leisure	passed		
singing	perishing		
summer	replied		
summertime	sing		
winter	spending		
	treasure		

"The Shepherd's Boy and the Wolf"

Moral: A liar will not be believed, even when he speaks the truth.

Specific Nouns (circle)	Descriptive Verbs (green)	Descriptive Adjectives (red)	Descriptive Adverbs (blue)
agony	brought	alarmed	last
assistance	crying	four	near
cause	destroyed	three	now
cries	help	whole	out
fear	killing		really
flock	lacerated		
heed	laughed		
leisure	paid		
neighbors	rendered		
pains	shouted		
terror	watched		
village			
villagers			

Treasure Island

Stated purpose of letter: "The ship is bought and fitted. She lies at anchor, ready for sea."

Specific Nouns (circle)	Descriptive Verbs (green)	Descriptive Adjectives (red)	Descriptive Adverbs (blue)
accident	bought	abominable	absurdly
adventures	cured	admirable	annoyingly
buccaneers	declare	country's	down
bull	declaring	fresh-water	full speed
calumnies	deny	high	literally

Diagnostic Prescriptive Services

nouns (circle)	verbs (green)	adjectives (red)	adverbs (blue)
class	discovered	honest	monstrously
company	eating	immortal	most
creature	engaged	indomitable	
crew	enjoy	magnificent	
fellow	fear	merest	
fortune	fell	odious	
French	fight	of importance	
friend	fitted		
frigate	hobbled	old	
glory	imagine	prejudiced	
	imagined	pretty	
health	kept	pure	
hitch	lies	ready	
length	look	remarkable	
management	lose	seafaring	
merits	lost	slow	
moment	proved	surprising	
native	regarded	sweeter	
pension	required	toughest	
pity	respect	transparent	
recommendation	showed	two-hundred	
riggers	slaved		
salts	sleeping		
schooner	sold		
service	touched		
smell	tramping		
sort	troubled		
spirit(s)	turned		
stroke			

nouns (circle)

swabs

tarpaulins

time

tons

treasure

tree

trifle

trump

"The Daffodils"

Specific Nouns (circle)	Descriptive Verbs (green)	Descriptive Adjectives (red)	Descriptive Adverbs (blue)
	*verbs used to describe the daffodils		
bay	*dancing	continuous	beneath
bliss	*fluttering	gay	beside
breeze	*outdid	golden	lonely
cloud	*stretched	inward	
company	*tossing	jocund	
couch	dance (ed) (s)	never-ending	
crowd	fills	of solitude	
daffodils	flash	pensive	
eye	floats	sparkling	
glance	gazed	sprightly	
glee	lie	ten thousand	
heads	saw	vacant	
heart	shine		

Diagnostic Prescriptive Services

nouns (circle)	verbs (green)
high	twinkle
hills	wandered
host	
lake	
line	
margin	
Milky Way	
mood	
pleasure	
poet	
show	
stars	
trees	
vales	
waves	
wealth	

"Paul Revere's Ride"

Specific Nouns (circle)	Descriptive Verbs (green)	Descriptive Adjectives (red)	Descriptive Adverbs (blue)
alarm	bends	alive	aghast
alders	bent	asleep	aloft
alley	blowing	bare	beneath
barking	borne	barrack	down
bay	burns	belfry	fearless
belfry arch	chasing	black	forevermore
belfry-chamber	climbed	blank	now
breath	creeping	bloody	out

nouns (circle)	verbs (green)	adjectives (red)	adverbs (blue)
bridge	crossed	booted	silently
British	crossing	broad	suddenly
Concord town	echo	country	wide
crowing	emerge	dead	
damp	felt		
darkness	fired	deep	
dread	fled	eager	
fate	floats	famous	
flock	flowing	farm-yard	
glare	flying	gilded	
gleam	galloped	heavy	
glimmer	gazed	highest	
gloom	gazes	huge	
grenadiers	hang	hurrying	
hoof-beats	hear (s)	impatient	
hurry	kindled	impetuous	
ladder	lay	lay	
land	lingers	lonely	
lantern	listen	loud	
light	look	measured	
man-of-war	lying	midnight	
mast	magnified	morning	
meadows	march	moving	
Medford town	mount	muffled	
message	mounted	of alarm	
moonlight	patted	of arms	
musket-ball	paused	of defiance	
muster	pierced	of fear	
Mystic	remembers	of feet	

nouns (circle)	verbs (green)	adjectives (red)
need	ride (s)	of shade
night-encampment	rises	opposite
		phantom
night-wind	rose	prison
North Church	rowed	ready
oar	skirt	rising
pebbles	spread	safe
perch	springs	secret
peril	stamped	sentinel's
prison bar	startled	shadowy
rafters	struck	signal
red-coats	swim	soft
reflection	swinging	sombre
Regulars	tightened	spectral
saddle-girth	turned	spurred
sea	waken	stealthy
search	walked	steep
shapes	wanders	still
silence	watches	tall
Somerset	widens	tranquil
spar	wrapped	trembling
spell		watchful
steed		wooden
tide		
tramp		
tread		
twitter		
weathercock		
work		

www.edudps.com

WRITE WITH THE BEST – Vol. 2

teaches the following genres:

WRITING POETRY
FREE VERSE
"The Railway Train"
by Emily Dickinson

WRITING A BUSINESS LETTER
To Sir John Everett Millais
Perkins Institution for the Blind
by Helen Keller

TAKING NOTES – WRITING OUTLINES –
WRITING SUMMARIES

WRITING ESSAYS
PERSUASIVE AND EXPOSITORY
"Common Sense" by Thomas Paine
"Of Studies" by Francis Bacon

WRITING A LITERARY CRITIQUE
AND A BOOK REVIEW

- **LITERARY CRITIQUE** by Edgar Allan Poe
of Nathaniel Hawthorne's *Twice-Told Tales*

- **BOOK REVIEW** by William Dean Howells
of Mark Twain's *The Adventures of Tom Sawyer*

WRITING A NEWSPAPER ARTICLE
"Would 'Treat 'Em Rough'"
by Ernest Hemingway

WRITING A SPEECH
"In Defense of Rabirius – Before the Senate"
by Marcus Tullius Cicero

WRITING A DRAMATIC MONOLOGUE
Mark Antony in *Julius Caesar*
by William Shakespeare

Diagnostic Prescriptive Services

www.edudps.com

OTHER PRODUCTS BY DPS   www.edudps.com

- Roots and Fruits A Comprehensive Vocabulary Curriculum covering Grades K through 12. This is a thirteen-year curriculum, starting at the kindergarten level. Contains 673 English forms of Greek and Latin roots and prefixes with their meanings, plus 1716 vocabulary words. It increases spelling, writing, dictionary and reading decoding skills. Contains most commonly tested words on the SAT (Scholastic Aptitude Test) as well as words from other standardized tests. Utilizes daily activities and games that appeal to all learning styles. Contains complete lesson plans. Vocabulary for the comprehension of all subjects including world and U.S. history, the sciences, foreign languages, mathematics and geometry, classical literature and reading, and the Bible. Takes as little as 15 minutes a day.

- The Diagnostic Prescriptive Assessment-Revised. This is a criterion referenced diagnostic test available in six separate assessments for grades K through 5. Each test is a 4-in-1 tool: (1) a diagnostic test (2) an effective pre-assessment for grade placement (3) provides objectives and scope & sequence for each grade level (4) serves as a yearly evaluation, portfolio, and Individual Educational Plan. • Thoroughly covers all required subjects • High criteria of mastery/Superior Educational Qualifications • No normed standards/True test scores • Grade Level Requirements. It is an excellent preparation tool for times when standardized testing is required. Each test was devised for parents to administer and score (answer key supplied) and comes with a remedial strategies section for correcting academic weaknesses. From 23 to 32 subtests- 51 to 65 pp.

- The Total Language Diagnostic Assessment with Remedial Strategies and Answer Key-Revised. This assessment is a compilation of the complete language subtests of The Diagnostic Prescriptive Assessment-Revised, K through 5th grades. Its unique features are: (a) A thorough workbook or manual for those who desire to work on language only-covering reading, phonics, reading vocabulary, reading comprehension, spelling, handwriting, composition, and dictionary and English skills. (b) A manual consisting only of actual test items of criterion referenced diagnostic tests. (c) Contains approximately 11 pages of remedial strategies *per grade level* for correcting academic weaknesses discovered through testing. (d) One student can use it for six years of academic requirements. (e) One manual can be used by a family with children ranging from K to 5th grades. It comes in two parts and contains 72 subtests-132 pp.

- The Concise Learning Styles Assessment with Instructional Guide. Determines the primary, second, and third level learning preferences, whether visual, auditory, or tactile/kinesthetic-for ages 7 through adult • comes complete with directions for administering and scoring • possesses grading scale for determination of "levels of strength" of each learning style • contains no "fluff" • includes instructional guide with teaching tips for each learning style • helps prevent misdiagnosis of learning problems • helps remove frustration and "burn-out" • can be used by the entire family.

- The Diagnostic Grade Placement Screening for grades K through 8. This assessment reveals the functional grade level of your child in reading decoding, math computation, and written expression for proper curriculum placement • Administered and scored by parents (grade key supplied).

- The Homeschooler's Guide For Learning Problems-Practical Tips For Daily Success is the only learning problems guide that we know of that has been written specifically for homeschoolers. Other books on the market deal with the student in a regular classroom setting. Our book contains a complete checklist for determining the specific learning problem of the student, as well as giving causes and solutions to the specific problems. It contains no superfluous material and was devised as a result of nineteen years of diagnosing and remediating learning difficulties.

- The Homeschooler's Guide To Attentional Difficulties-Practical Tips For Daily Success. Covers subjects such as ADHD-Fact or Fiction? How do I know if it is an attentional problem or another problem? • Takes a non-medication approach to solve attentional problems • Practical modifications to make for your child which will alter his learning experience • Doesn't contain "fluff", but rather gets right to the issues involved • Contains "Real Life" success stories of homeschooled children • Answers the most frequently asked questions about attentional problems • Comes complete with practical guidelines for teaching each subject and dealing with attentional problems at home and away from home.